Western Star Publishing

Books

By

Arlene Millman

Boomerang - A Miracle Trilogy

3/22/03

Dear Lois,
Wish you love +
miracles forever!
∞
Arlene

Boomerang - A Miracle Trilogy: The Tale
of a Remarkable Boston Terrier

By

Arlene Millman

Western Star Publishing LLC
P.O. Box 5263
Cheyenne, Wyoming 82003

Boomerang - A Miracle Trilogy

A Western Star Publishing Book / Published by arrangements
with the author

Printing history
First printing by Western Star Publishing 2002

All rights reserved by Western Star Publishing

Copyright 2002
Arlene Millman

ISBN# 1-932245-01-4

Western Star Publishing

BOOMERANG - A MIRACLE TRILOGY

by

Arlene Millman

1

Book One: Boomerang - A Miracle

Book Two: Boomerang - A Miracle Encore

Book Three: Boomerang - A Miracle Odyssey

BOOMERANG - A MIRACLE

An Inspirational Tale

by

Arlene Millman

A miracle is an event which creates faith.
This is the purpose and nature of miracles.

--George Bernard Shaw

Boomerang — A Miracle Trilogy

MISSION STATEMENT

My purpose in writing the BOO-MERANG TRILOGY was to inspire, inform and entertain. It is my fervent wish to imbue you, the reader, with a sense of hope within the present context...and for the future as well.

As an ageless inspirational tale, the book is a rare and unique combination of spiritual insight and stimulating exploration. I sincerely believe that: Through love, all things are possible, including miracles! I also believe that, indeed, kindness is contagious!

BOOMERANG is the answer, for those of you seeking comfort and reassurance in our ever-changing, technologically oriented world. The BOOMERANG TRILOGY is naturally linked to the increasing spiritual consciousness associated with the onset of both the third millennium and the 21st century.

The message is a universal one. Everybody needs to believe in the power of

Boomerang — A Miracle Trilogy

love to heal and create miracles!* Everybody can learn to see with their heart, what may be invisible to their eyes....

May reading this book transform your life forever.

*Miracle, by definition, is any wonderful or amazing thing, fact or event.

Boomerang — A Miracle Trilogy

CONTENTS

Dedication
Acknowledgments
Poem
Prologue

Epilogue

Message from the Author

Boomerang's Message

In Loving Memory of

IMPERIAL'S BOOMERANG MIRACLE

May his story help all those who have lost a cherished pet, whether young or old. The unconditional love we share with our pets is so strong, it cannot be destroyed by space or time; as long as we hold their memory close to our hearts. Through love, all things are possible.

ACKNOWLEDGMENTS

A special thank you to Dr. Alan Coren, of West Hills Animal Hospital, for his extraordinary efforts and loving care on behalf of Boomerang. Dr. Coren's concern and treatment both enhanced the quality and extended the length of Boomerang's life, well past what might have been expected. My sincere gratitude to Dr. Coren and his devoted staff, for their kindness and support.

Heartfelt appreciation to Susan Marino, creator of Angel's Gate; Wendie Grossman, bereavement counselor at Bide-A-Wee; Medea Berkman, facilitator for Paw to Heart. In the grief filled days following Boomerang's untimely passing, their support and understanding helped me come to terms with the pain. They were empathetic catalysts, offering encouragement and suggestions. I began keeping a journal to help the healing process and commit my feelings to paper. The writing sessions were therapeutic, and this inspirational tale about the miracle of Boomerang evolved from the ashes of my grief. Further information about these dedicated individuals and the resources available can be found at the end of this trilogy, in the Appendix.

Boomerang — A Miracle Trilogy

A TRIBUTE TO BOOMERANG

Born on a beautiful summer day
He arrived from a place far, far away
Boomerang was his chosen name
My life changed, never to be the same.

His heart was filled to the brim with love
He was indeed a miracle, sent from above
When he became sick, I cried inside
By some miracle, he survived the rough ride.

His life continued for awhile
Just his presence made me smile
The doctor said he could not stay
I adored him, continued to hope and pray.

In my heart, I knew he would not last
He was an angel, a gift from the past
More precious than diamonds, platinum or gold
Boomerang was a blessing, a miracle to behold.

When the time came to say good-bye
He departed Earth, but did not die
His soul still sends me unconditional love
Someday he'll return from that place up above.

11

PROLOGUE

The following is an inspirational tale, based upon the life of Boomerang. He was a tiny little dog, with a tremendously big heart, and a mission to fulfill.

His presence on Earth was indeed a miracle! And so, the amazing story of Boomerang begins to unfold....

14

Boomerang — A Miracle Trilogy

Part 1

Destined DE-but

Let us follow our destiny, ebb and flow.
Whatever may happen, we master fortune
by accepting it.

--Virgil

15

ONE

Boomerang's life was indeed a miracle! A special little bundle of pure love, who was born on a beautiful summer day in July. He was a tiny, black, brindle and white Boston Terrier, weighing less than eight ounces. Boomerang had chosen his name, prior to his arrival on Earth.

To let everybody know his name, he came with a special type of label. On the very top of his head was the definite shape of a boomerang. It was an unmistakable black outline on his pure white blaze, almost as if he had been stamped with indelible ink. The name seemed to suit him so perfectly. And so, it was decided that Boomerang would be his official name.

Everybody was extremely excited about the new puppy in the household. There was Grandpa Gem, Mommy Crystal and Sister Penelope, who were also Boston Terriers. Of course, there was also his human mommy and daddy. They all thought he was the cutest, smartest, most adorable puppy they had ever seen. And, he even came pre-named!

His human mommy and daddy took many pictures of him, on the day he was born. They planned on taking many more photos of Boomerang, as he grew, so they could capture the memories of his puppyhood and place them in a special photo album.

Boomerang's eyes were still sealed closed, so he could not see his family yet. But, he felt surrounded by so much love, on this first day of his life. He felt very lucky to be born into such a wonderful family. Contentment and joy filled his entire being. He wondered what new excitement tomorrow would bring.

TWO

As the days passed, Boomerang did not gain weight and grow the way a normal healthy puppy is supposed to. In fact, he lost weight, and he became tinier than ever. When he was exactly one week old, he be-

Boomerang — A Miracle Trilogy

came very sick. His human mommy and daddy rushed him to the animal hospital. They were very worried and not sure what to expect. By some miracle, he survived!

One morning, when Boomerang was two weeks and two days old, his eyes finally opened. He could now see his entire Boston Terrier family: Grandpa Gem, Mommy Crystal and Sister Penelope. He also saw his human mommy and daddy for the first time. Everything and everybody looked so beautiful to him.

He felt so fortunate. He was lucky to be alive, and he had his whole life ahead of him. There was so much to see and do. He had so much to learn. Boomerang's mind was filled with questions. He knew the answers would come, in time. Meanwhile, he would be patient and wait.

THREE

The following week, Boomerang became very sick again. He was rushed back to the animal hospital. They kept him

19

for what seemed like a very long time. Eventually, he was strong enough to come home. He had survived again. It was indeed a miracle!

He was so happy to be home. His family taught him to how to walk again. Eventually, he learned how to run and jump and play. As his puppy teeth came in, he learned how to chew and eat solid food. He learned how to drink water out of a bowl, without dribbling too badly. Boomerang was curious about going up and down steps, but he was much too little to try. That lesson would have to wait until he was older.

Boomerang grew bigger and stronger, with each passing day. His Boston Terrier family were very happy with their new addition. His human mommy and daddy were so relieved that he was now a normal, healthy puppy. They bought him all sorts of toys and playthings. They took pictures of him almost every day, to place in his special photo album. Everybody relaxed, and they looked forward to a bright and happy future for little Boomerang. The crisis was finally over, and life in the household could return to normal.

FOUR

During the next few months, Boomerang went to the veterinarian for the usual series of routine puppy visits. He loved seeing all his friends at the animal hospital. He had made many friends during his previous stays at the hospital, and everybody made such a fuss when he came back to visit. They would hug him and kiss him, so he felt very special. Some of the women would kiss him right on the top of his white blaze and leave a big red lipstick mark. He did not mind. It made him feel so filled with love.

He especially loved seeing his favorite veterinarian, Dr. C., and let him know it by kissing him on the nose. He would try to entertain Dr. C. and make him laugh. It was the least he could do. After all, Dr. C. had saved his life. It had been a miracle, but Dr. C. had helped. Boomerang was so grateful to Dr. C. and thankful to be alive.

Boomerang loved life. He lived and experienced every day to the fullest, spreading joy and love wherever possible. Boomerang came into this life with a very special talent -- bringing out the best in those whose lives he touched. He shared his enthusiasm with everybody. His love was equally contagious.

Boomerang knew how to have fun, and he thrived on entertaining an audience. He was a natural. It soon became apparent that the name he had chosen, prior to his birth, was so appropriate. People would say, "what a cute name -- Boomerang," and then would chuckle.

This pleased Boomerang and made him very happy. He loved people, and it naturally followed that he loved to make them feel happy. This was his purpose.

He also had a talent for making eye contact with people, as a way of communicating his feelings and conveying mes-

Boomerang — A Miracle Trilogy

sages. He would look someone straight in the eye, with his huge brown eyes, and wait for a response. He would watch their body language. Then he would decide how best to entertain them. Sometimes, if they were lucky, he would fetch one of his favorite toys, stand it up at their feet, and get into play position with his head down and his rump up in the air. Then he would wait for the fun and games to begin. Boomerang became quite an expert at playing, and he was enjoying life to the fullest.

FIVE

Boomerang was a very, very wise little puppy. He just seemed to know things, from the time he was born. He did not even know how he knew, he just did. His Grandpa Gem also taught him many important things about life and people.

Boomerang admired Grandpa Gem's wisdom and patience so much. Of course, Grandpa Gem had acquired these traits over many, many years of experience.

Boomerang could not even imagine being that old. Grandpa Gem had lived on Earth for over fourteen years, before Boomerang was born. That was equal to over one hundred human years. That was amazing!

Boomerang loved his Grandpa Gem very much, and told him so every day. This made Grandpa Gem so happy. He was very proud to have a grandson like Boomerang. Every night, before they went to sleep, Grandpa Gem told Boomerang how much he loved him, and that he would always watch over and protect him.

Boomerang felt so lucky to be surrounded by so much love. He wanted to share this feeling with everybody, so they could be this happy too. That would be his purpose, for as long as he lived -- to give unconditional love.

Even as a young puppy, Boomerang knew how to see with his heart, as well as his eyes. He could naturally analyze a situation and come to the rescue with just the appropriate version of his unconditional love. Whether it was a youngster with a

24

bruise, or an adult in a state of depression, Boomerang used his special brand of love to save the day. He could ease the pain of a bruise with a series of snuggles and sincere kisses applied to the appropriate place. When he encountered a senior adult who was sad and lonely, Boomerang would envelope them in the warmth of his aura. Sometimes, he would impulsively jump into someone's lap and cuddle up, sending them good vibes. Other times, he would shower them with tender little kisses that tickled, until the lucky recipient would eventually respond with a smile. Boomerang didn't give up on anybody. He was persistent with his loving, and the formula seemed to work well.

If his favorite Dr. C. was out of sorts with a headache, Boomerang knew exactly what to do. First he would concentrate and send him the most loving thoughts possible. Then he placed his two front paws around Dr. C.s neck, while he ever so gently planted kisses along his furrowed brow and down his temples, finally stopping at the ears. Eventually Boomerang could see the tension ease and the headache go away. Even Dr. C. thought Boomerang's powers of perception were truly amazing.

Boomerang innately understood the power of love to heal, and he wondered why more people didn't use such an untapped power for the greater good of mankind. When I grow up, he resolved, I will teach others the power of love to heal both physical and emotional pain. And as far as he was concerned, love could create miracles that were inexplicable in logical terms. That's one of the reasons I'm here on Earth, he reasoned, and I am ever so grateful.

Boomerang never took his innate talents for granted. In fact, the more his awareness grew, the more humble he became. He was a natural at dealing with people, and he appreciated the gift. He knew in his heart that the more love you share and give, the more love you have to give. And so, he unselfishly shared his gift of love with all those who were fortunate enough to know him. The love that flowed from Boomerang's pure heart was strong, steady and unconditional.

Wow! I'm so lucky, he thought, to be blessed with such a wonderful gift from the universe. I promise to use it wisely and appropriately, he resolved to himself. Boomerang was indeed a very wise little puppy.

Part 2

Delightful DE-velopment

Everything flows, nothing stays still. Nothing is permanent, but change.

-- Heraclitus (ca. 500 BC)

SIX

Boomerang's life continued uneventfully for awhile. He enjoyed being at home, surrounded by his family. He could spend hours playing with Grandpa Gem, Mommy Crystal and Sister Penelope. He also loved to spend time with his human mommy and daddy. They would all cuddle on the couch, and watch amusing programs on television. He would receive dozens of hugs and kisses every day. He never tired of all this attention. He knew they all loved him very much, and the feeling was mutual.

Boomerang also appreciated being outside, communicating with nature. Although his favorite outdoor pastimes were sniffing flowers and watching butterflies, he was also amused by the other creatures he saw in his yard. There were rabbits nibbling on the grass, squirrels playing tag in the trees, and chipmunks scurrying around the garden. He also watched the many varieties of birds flying overhead and building nests. Occasionally, when he gazed up at the sky, he would see a beautiful rainbow. He considered it absolutely magical, and he would be overjoyed. Rainbows were such a rare and special treat for Boomerang. He thought their beauty was breathtaking!

Boomerang thought all of nature was a wonderful sight to behold. Sometimes, at night, he even managed to see raccoons, and he definitely heard the distant hoot of an owl. Boomerang was very observant, and his hearing was impeccable.

Wherever he went, he noticed everything and listened to everything. That is how he learned so quickly. He wanted to become wise, just like his Grandpa Gem.

Sometimes, on the weekends, his human mommy and daddy took him to very special places, like the park and the duck pond. Once, he even went to the harbor, to see the water and the boats. That is where he saw his first sea gull, and several smaller birds called terns. They were very different from the birds in his yard. It was

32

all so interesting.

Of course, Boomerang made new friends wherever he went. People would stop, and they would ask if they could pet him and take his picture. He loved the attention, and he enjoyed making new friends. He was accustomed to having his picture taken, since his human mommy and daddy had been taking photos of him since the day he was born. He would patiently pose for the camera, and he was glad it made people happy. Fortunately, he had learned the lesson of patience from his Grandpa Gem. He was very thankful to be blessed with a wise and loving grandpa. How lucky could a puppy get?

Soon, there were many albums filled with Boomerang's pictures, and people loved to look at them. They would smile, and that made him happy. There was even a photo of him placed in the very center of the bulletin board, at his veterinarian's office. He considered that to be such an honor. It made him love his favorite veterinarian, Dr. C., even more, if that was possible. Boomerang was scheduled to visit Dr. C. the following week, and he looked forward to the appointment with great anticipation!

SEVEN

It was a delightful fall day in November. The air was getting cooler, and the leaves on the trees were turning from green into the whole palette of autumn colors. Boomerang found this to be fascinating. He was almost four months old, and he was filled with curiosity about the world around him. His imagination was very active, and the future was filled with infinite possibilities.

When Boomerang arrived for his appointment at the veterinarian's office, he was greeted warmly by all of his friends. They were so happy to see him, and everybody welcomed him lovingly with hugs and kisses. He seemed strong and healthy, and he weighed almost ten pounds. That in itself was cause for celebration. His favorite veterinarian, Dr. C., was quite pleased with his progress and thought he looked great! Boomerang was so happy, he gave Dr. C. a big wet kiss on his nose. Dr. C. chuckled in response and kissed Boomerang on the top of his head. They certainly had mutual respect and affection for each other.

Dr. C. informed Boomerang's human mommy that he was finally big enough for some tests that were previously postponed, because he had been much too little. It was just a precaution, and nothing to be concerned about.

Meanwhile, Boomerang and his human mommy said good-bye to everybody. They did not expect to return for a while, since this was his last scheduled puppy visit. However, such was not the case.

The test results indicated an internal problem, that had been caused when he was a sick little puppy. Dr. C. suggested a plan of treatment, and everybody hoped for the best.

Boomerang was put on a special

diet. At first, it tasted very different. But, he adjusted well, and he eventually learned to enjoy his new food and ate with much enthusiasm. Boomerang also had special medicine that he was given every morning and every night. It was supposed to be good for him, so he cooperated fully and swallowed the pills.

He appreciated all the special care he was receiving. Everybody was making such a fuss over him, and he really enjoyed all the attention. However, he also felt badly that all the people he loved were so worried about him. He wanted to cheer up everybody, so they would be happy again. That was his purpose -- to spread joy and happiness. And so, he was determined to get better. By some miracle, he seemed to thrive on his special diet, his special medicine, and all the special loving attention. He was filled with a special energy that only love can create.

As the weeks passed, Boomerang grew bigger and stronger. He now weighed twelve pounds. He had gained over two pounds in less than a month. They called it a growth spurt. Everybody was so happy. It was time for a celebration! His human mommy and daddy decided to plan a one-half birthday party for Boomerang.

EIGHT

It was a remarkably beautiful winter day in January. Boomerang was exactly six months old. He had lived on Earth for half a year. That meant today was his one-half birthday. They were going to celebrate with a big party for all his friends and family. It was going to be so much fun. He would probably get to pose for pictures, and receive many hugs and kisses. He would enjoy every minute of it, because hugs and kisses were the best way to give and receive love.

Before the party that day, his human mommy had a big surprise for Boomerang. She explained they were going to a dog boutique, so he could choose his own special one-half birthday present. When they arrived at the boutique, Boomerang started to explore the many possibilities.

Across the room, he observed a beautiful black patent leather pet carrier with leopard print trim. He walked over to investigate further. He sniffed it first. Then he circled around it. Finally he walked inside and curled up. The floor was so soft and fluffy he imagined he was floating on a cloud. It had the most comfortable imitation lambskin rug inside, and there was plenty of room for him to stand up and turn around. It was perfect! He had made his choice. The Sherpa bag, as it was called, would be his special one-half birthday present.

Not only was his new carrier comfortable, but it was also practical. Since Boomerang was fortunate enough to travel in the car almost every day, it would be a safe place for him to ride. The carrier could even be attached to the seat belt in the car, for additional security. He felt very protected and loved. Boomerang was having a wonderful one-half birthday!

Happily, his human mommy had planned another surprise for him. The trip to the dog boutique was the perfect opportunity for Boomerang to choose his winter wardrobe. This shopping expedition was turning out to be even more fun than Boomerang expected. There were so many beautiful items. Eventually, Boomerang chose his three favorites: a shiny orange rain slicker with a hood; a black and red plaid polar fleece winter coat; a red turtleneck sweater, with a yellow, blue and green swirl pattern.

Boomerang loved bright colors, and everything fit him perfectly. He was looking forward to the first snow of winter. Now he was outfitted and ready. He had heard so much about snow, he was really excited about seeing it and playing in it for the first time in his life.

Boomerang appreciated every moment of his special one-half birthday celebration. He was filled with contentment and joy. That night, while he slept, he dreamed about snowflakes in the air.

NINE

When the first snow came that winter, Boomerang ran outside to look at it. The snow was beautiful, just as Grandpa Gem had promised. Grandpa Gem had also told him that snow was made from an infinite amount of snowflakes, and that no two snowflakes were ever the same. Boomerang thought it was fascinating, and he was so glad Grandpa Gem took the time to teach him. Everyday, Grandpa Gem would spend hours with Boomerang, explaining how things always worked out for the best, and sharing the knowledge and wisdom he had acquired during his life on Earth. Boomerang trusted his grandpa totally, and he listened intently to everything Grandpa Gem said. They were very close and devoted to one another. Their bond was based on mutual love and admiration.

Boomerang and his entire family went out to play in the snow, as more snowflakes continued to float down from the sky. He jumped and ran and played in it. He even tasted it. He was happy, and he appreciated the whole new experience in his life. It was quite cold outside, but he did not feel it. He was wearing his new red turtleneck sweater, with the yellow, blue and green swirls. He felt toasty warm. Of course, his human mommy and daddy thought this was the perfect opportunity to take more pictures of him playing in the snow in his new red sweater. They took dozens of pictures to put in his special photo album.

Eventually, the grass was completely covered by a beautiful white blanket of snow. It looked so pure. Boomerang loved the way it glistened in the sunlight. If he stood in just the right place, he could see his very own shadow, outlined on the snowy ground below. His little feet left paw prints wherever he walked, and it was fun making paw patterns in the freshly fallen snow.

The whole day had been fantastic!

It was better than anything he could have imagined. Boomerang hoped he would get to play in the snow many more times that winter. And so he did.

Part 3

Deep DE-votion

The best and most beautiful things in the world cannot be seen or even touched. They must be felt with the heart.

-- Helen Keller

Boomerang — A Miracle Trilogy

TEN

Less than a month later, Grandpa Gem told Boomerang that he was being summoned to Heaven, and he would be leaving Earth very soon to become an angel. Grandpa Gem assured Boomerang he would always protect and love him. He explained that he would be watching over him at all times, although Boomerang would not be able to see him. He promised Boomerang that their bond was so strong it could never be broken by space or time.

Grandpa Gem told Boomerang that this separation was only temporary. One day they would be reunited again, but until then, Boomerang needed to be strong. Boomerang had complete faith in Grandpa Gem's wisdom. He trusted his grandpa completely and loved him dearly. Boomerang promised Grandpa Gem that he would try his best to make him proud, and continue with his purpose of spreading unconditional love and happiness.

Grandpa Gem departed Earth, as

planned, on a cold and crisp winter morning. It was a unique and peaceful transition. Grandpa Gem was glowing with the warmth of contentment as he contemplated his blissful future in Heaven.

Boomerang missed Grandpa Gem very much. However, he was satisfied knowing that Grandpa Gem would always be there whenever he needed him, and would love him forever. That made Boomerang feel happy and protected. Boomerang also knew he could rely on Grandpa Gem's solemn promise. Someday, they would be together again, and they would love each other forever and ever.

And so, Boomerang kept his promise to Grandpa Gem. He reviewed their lessons with care and concentrated on following his grandpa's suggestions. Of course, it would be a while before Boomerang would realize the full extent of his powers. Grandpa Gem had always encouraged him to open up his heart chakra and give love freely and unconditionally. Boomerang's heart was so big and his soul so pure, that he had the ability to see the pain and hurt in others. Love is the strongest force on Earth, he thought to himself. I can overcome negative thoughts and feelings with the power of my unconditional love. And, with this contribution, I will assist people in becoming more happy and productive. I can help heal the scars that impair the functioning of a wounded heart and make someone whole again.

Boomerang thought a great deal about how he could apply the quality of unconditional love to enhance the lives of others. He was in tune with his inner voice, and he felt confident the universe would show him the way. He knew from experience that emotional pain could be far greater than physical pain. So, when he encountered someone with an emptiness inside and a lonely heart, he immediately sent them the healing rays of love. The response was usually swift and that gave him great pleasure, knowing he had rescued a broken heart. When he sent out strong feelings of love to another being, the intrin-

47

sic healing quality seemed to be absorbed exactly where it was most needed. For example, a broken heart became whole again, and a forlorn expression turned around into the hint of a smile and then a broad grin. Boomerang thought to himself, it is so amazing that I can change a person's outlook and enhance their life with a generous dose of unconditional love! But, it was really more than that. Upon further analysis, Boomerang realized they perceived his sincere caring as a validation of their own worth, and it changed their self-image. The world took on a rosy glow, thanks to a little assistance from a remarkable Boston Terrier. A sprinkling of pure love and kindness can make all the difference. Boomerang had learned his lessons well.

He knew Grandpa Gem would be so proud of his unselfish deeds. He smiled to himself with satisfaction, while Grandpa Gem smiled down upon him from the heavenly plane. You've learned your lessons astoundingly well, my boy. I am so very proud of you. Boomerang looked up and felt Grandpa Gem's love flow over and through him, bathing him in a protective glow of heavenly light.

ELEVEN

Before Boomerang knew it, winter was over and spring had arrived. Squirrels were scampering across the lawn. Chipmunks were playing tag, and frogs were hopping in the garden. Flowers were blooming in all his favorite colors of the rainbow. Everything looked beautiful.

Boomerang thought springtime was glorious. He loved spring! There was so much joy in his heart. He decided to celebrate spring every day. The possibilities for fun were endless.

Boomerang was now more than nine months old, and he was finally fully grown. He actually weighed fourteen pounds. People still thought he was a cute little puppy, but he no longer considered himself little. Boomerang was the biggest he would ever be, and he was definitely cute. When the tip of his little pink tongue would stick just a tiny bit out of his mouth, he looked even cuter. He did this frequently when he was concentrating, relaxing or daydreaming. Sometimes his little pink tongue would appear while he was asleep, which enhanced his cuteness even further. Boomerang was a very appealing little dog, both in appearance and behaviour. He had a distinctive expression and a winning personality that everybody loved.

He was going to the veterinarian more often now for tests and special treatments. He understood, and he loved riding in the car in his special carrier. That was such a treat. He knew everybody loved him, and that they wanted him to get better. Everybody at the animal hospital was very concerned, especially his favorite veterinarian Dr. C. They were all doing their best to keep him healthy for as long as possible.

He continued on his special diet, which he really enjoyed eating. He was given additional medicine as a preventative measure. Boomerang had learned to swallow pills very well. Now there was a new liquid medicine he needed everyday to keep him feeling well. He always appreciated all the care he received, and he always reciprocated with unconditional love.

Boomerang continued to enjoy all the incredible wonders of spring. He wished Grandpa Gem was there to share it with him. But he knew Grandpa Gem was watching over him, and he always felt Grandpa Gem's love and protection around him.

Boomerang was constantly surrounded by his family and friends, who loved him very much. That love nourished him, and gave him the extra strength he needed. He lived life to the fullest, and continued to concentrate on his purpose. It was indeed a miracle!

TWELVE

Soon it would be Boomerang's first birthday. He had lived for twelve miraculous months on Earth, and experienced all four seasons. The cycle was about to be completed, and a major celebration was planned.

Finally, the day arrived. Once again it was a beautiful summer day in July. Only this was a very special day. All his family and friends wanted to share this extra special day with him. There were so very many guests, and he was the center of attention. In fact, he was the guest of honor. There were wonderful decorations and colorful balloons, and so many birthday presents. He was very excited and having so much fun. Every day of his life just seemed to get better and better. He was having a great time.

The birthday cake was enormous, and it was covered with more candles than he could count. The top of the cake was made of smooth, white whipped cream. The inscription was written with dark brown chocolate letters, and it said: "We Love You Boomerang. Happy First Birthday. May All Your Wishes Come True."

This sentiment was so beautiful he

wanted to cry. Instead he took a deep breath, blew out all the candles, and made a special wish. As usual, his human mommy and daddy took many pictures to keep in his special photo album.

THIRTEEN

Of course, every day was a celebration of life and love for Boomerang. It naturally followed that he received presents all the time, from his friends and family. They gave him presents because he was such a good dog, and because he spread joy and gave them the best gift of all -- unconditional love.

One day Boomerang received a new toy that was to become his favorite. It was made of red, yellow and white latex, and there was a squeaker inside. The name on the front said "BIG KAHUNA" in bold blue letters. In the state of Hawaii, the Kahuna is someone with a vast knowledge.

By now, Boomerang had acquired so many toys. He loved to play with all of them, but he had such a special attachment to his Big Kahuna. It was as if they were made for each other. He slept with it at night, and he took it with him wherever he went. Boomerang's affinity for Big Kahuna was heartwarming, and also quite understandable. They were both very little. They were a great deal alike. They represented a vast amount of knowledge. Soon, Boomerang's nickname became Big Kahuna. It was an acknowledgment of the wisdom and knowledge he had acquired during his life.

FOURTEEN

Boomerang's human mommy and daddy were very proud of him. They were so glad that Boomerang was a wise and happy little dog, and they loved him very much. They also admired his courage and determination. His human mommy and daddy felt so blessed by his unconditional love, they would do anything for him. They made a solemn promise to Boomerang. They would do everything they could to make him better.

His human mommy and daddy were totally devoted to him, and determined to find help. They called and consulted with specialists all over the country, seeking a cure for Boomerang. But despite all their efforts, nobody could find a permanent solution for Boomerang's problem. They tried to heal him with the best treatments available. But there was no cure, only hope.

They continued to shower Boomerang with enormous amounts of love and attention, while hoping for a miracle.

Part 4

Dearest DE-termination

The butterfly counts not months,
but moments, and has time enough.

-- Rabindranath Tagore

FIFTEEN

Despite every effort, Boomerang eventually became sicker. Over many months, he repeatedly relapsed and recovered. Every time he bounced back, he demonstrated how he truly lived up to his name -- Boomerang. It was the name he had chosen for himself before being born. He was a determined little dog; a miraculous little creature with a purpose.

As time passed, Boomerang would get sick, and then get better again. He was very determined to survive. His mission on Earth, to spread love and joy, had not been completed. His little body might be getting weaker, but his mind and spirit were strong, so strong he bounced back time and time again, ready to begin anew.

He still had much more to share. Especially with his human mommy and daddy, and all his friends at the animal hospital. He always loved to visit with his favorite veterinarian, Dr. C. As Boomerang became sicker, he had to go to the animal hospital more often, but he never minded because he loved everybody there. He loved to visit all his friends at the animal hospital and spread his special brand of love and joy. They were his audience, and this was a perfect opportunity to entertain them and cheer them up, especially Dr. C. Boomerang always remembered that Dr. C. had helped save his life, and he would be eternally grateful.

SIXTEEN

Fall and winter seemed to pass quickly for Boomerang. Before he knew it, spring had arrived. He loved spring even more than he did last year. It was a time of birth and new beginnings. Flowers were blooming and birds were chirping. Baby bunny rabbits were nibbling on the grass. The trees were sprouting new green leaves on their formerly bare branches. Everything around him was so fresh and alive.

The world was a beautiful place, and Boomerang felt quite content. He con-

Boomerang — A Miracle Trilogy

tinued to enjoy an excellent quality of life. He took great pleasure in spending most of his time at home, with its comfortable couches, soft beds and plentiful supply of toys. He particularly loved his yard, where he could run and play, sniffing the delicious fragrance of the colorful flowers, and watching the beautiful butterflies. There was something about a butterfly that he truly admired. He was not certain what it was, but he knew for sure that someday he would find the answer.

Boomerang would bark when necessary to defend his territory, just the way Grandpa Gem had taught him. It was one of Boomerang's responsibilities, to protect his household. But mostly he communicated with others through his heart and soul. His big, brown eyes had a powerful effect on most people. They were both magnetic and hypnotic. His deep-set eyes were the windows of his soul. They were intense in expression, and they were filled with the wisdom of the ages. When you looked into his eyes for just a moment, you could get a brief glimpse of his beautiful soul. If you were very fortunate, you could actually lose yourself in its depths.

SEVENTEEN

It was a lovely spring day. Boomerang was finally coming home from the animal hospital where he had been for almost one week. To celebrate the occasion, his human mommy and daddy planned a special surprise for him. They were taking him shopping for a very unusual "welcome home" present -- a butterfly bush of his very own.

Butterfly bushes are formally known as buddleia. Butterflies are attracted to the bright colors of their tubular shaped flowers, which bloom from mid-spring through fall. They also like the strong fragrance of the flower nectar, which is their primary food source.

Boomerang rode in the car, in his special carrier, to the local garden nursery. He was so surprised and excited. The nurs-

Boomerang — A Miracle Trilogy

ery had a large selection of buddleia from which to choose. There were butterfly bushes in all shades of pink, purple, lavender, as well as white. Boomerang thought they were all beautiful. With the help of his human mommy and daddy, he chose a butterfly bush with large clusters of deep purple flowers. It was called a Black Knight buddleia, and Boomerang hoped the plentiful flowers would attract many varieties of butterflies. They all went home to plant the new bush in the garden.

Boomerang was so happy with his new butterfly bush. He could watch it grow, and now he would have even more butterflies to watch. What an exciting thought. He took great delight in observing the various butterflies as they came fluttering into his yard. He loved the colors and patterns on their wings. He could watch them and study their graceful movements for hours.

Butterflies were still a mystery to Boomerang. He found them to be fascinating, but they also represented so many unanswered questions. That evening he went to sleep dreaming of beautiful butterflies.

EIGHTEEN

Boomerang felt so fortunate to have such a wonderful family. They loved him and were always telling him how special he was. In return, he would be the best dog he could possibly be, and continue spreading unconditional love. Every morning, when he awoke, Boomerang anticipated the future with his own unique blend of enthusiasm and wisdom. He looked forward to another delightful day, when he could share his special message of joy and love.

He was a powerful influence on everybody whose lives he touched. By setting a daily example, he taught people the power and the purpose of love. He raised their awareness with his very presence. Boomerang left a permanent legacy, by inspiring others to perceive life as a miraculous experience.

He thought the world was a won-

Boomerang — A Miracle Trilogy

derful place, and life offered so many marvelous opportunities. Boomerang truly appreciated the miracle of every moment of his life on Earth. It was amazing to behold his tremendous courage, his boundless joy, and most of all, his unconditional love.

Boomerang loved just for the sake of loving, and he expected nothing in return. His gratification came purely from giving. The more he gave, the more he rejoiced. Sometimes so much happiness filled his tremendously big heart, he thought it would burst from sheer joy.

Boomerang — A Miracle Trilogy

Part 5

Deliberate DE-cision

Energy is eternal delight.

-- William Blake

NINETEEN

Time passed and Boomerang continued to enjoy his life on Earth with his family, friends and playmates. His quality of life was very good. He had become quite an expert at kissing and cuddling, and he loved to sleep in bed with his human mommy and daddy. It was a privilege that he had earned. Every night he would look forward to snuggling up in the soft bed and having beautiful dreams.

One night, while he was asleep, a Guardian Angel visited Boomerang. The angel told him that he was such a good dog, he had completed his mission on Earth much sooner than expected. He was now eligible to become an angel.

It was a terribly difficult choice. Boomerang was really torn. He loved his family and friends on Earth. He did not wish to leave them. But he also felt excited about the prospect of becoming an angel, and being reunited with his Grandpa Gem. He loved his Grandpa Gem dearly, and he missed him very much.

His life on Earth had been full and rewarding, with his human mommy and daddy, his Boston Terrier family, and all his wonderful friends. He had experienced love to the fullest, and he had reciprocated totally, with all the unconditional love in his heart and soul.

In his infinite wisdom Boomerang knew the time was right. He was ready. And so the decision was made.

TWENTY

Boomerang was scheduled to make the transition and become an angel. The journey began in June, exactly twenty-three months after he had been born. It was a beautiful summer day, just as when he arrived on Earth.

A feeling of euphoria gently swept over Boomerang. He felt a sensation of unlimited freedom as he had never experienced before. He was gliding, just like a butterfly. Suddenly he realized why he always admired butterflies so much. Of course they were fun to watch, and they were beautiful. But more important, butterflies were the "symbols of the soul."

Boomerang felt a sudden rush of energy. The next thing he knew, he was soaring through fluffy white clouds up to Heaven. He thought the entire journey was absolutely incredible. He was ecstatic!

When Boomerang arrived in Heaven, Grandpa Gem was there to welcome him, precisely as he had promised. Grandpa Gem looked young and handsome, just like the pictures Boomerang had seen of him in the special photo album back on Earth. They greeted each other lovingly and joyously. They hugged and kissed each other for a very long time. Then Grandpa Gem introduced Boomerang to all his friends in Heaven, and showed him all the wonderful rewards waiting for him.

There were all of his favorite toys, including Big Kahuna. There were spectacular gardens for him to run and play in.

71

The gardens were filled with brightly colored flowers of different shapes and sizes. There were the most beautiful butterflies that Boomerang had ever seen, fluttering in the air, and butterfly bushes everywhere. There were glistening snowflakes and breathtaking rainbows. There was even an endless supply of comfortable couches and soft beds full of pillows.

Everything was magnificent. It was all so amazing! Boomerang had become an angel. He had earned his wings. He could watch over all his loved ones back on Earth. He could even visit them, although they would not actually see him. His life on Earth had been of short duration, but it had been perfect, and filled with so much love. Most important, he had fulfilled his mission. The special wish he had made last year on his birthday had come true.

Boomerang was very happy and at peace. His life was indeed a miracle! It was the best life he could ever have wished for. He would always treasure the memories.

Boomerang — A Miracle Trilogy

And someday, if he chose to, he could return to Earth on another mission. Meanwhile, he would have fun and enjoy being an angel. This was a whole new beginning for Boomerang.

THE END

EPILOGUE

This story is a special tribute to Boomerang. His presence on Earth was a blessing to all those whose lives he touched. He accepted his fate with dignity, ease and especially love. He was indeed a miracle to behold!

Both Boomerang and his beloved grandfather Gem are interred in a peaceful sanctuary at the Bide-A-Wee Pet Memorial Park. The appropriate literal translation of Bide-A-Wee means, "stay awhile."

A portion of the proceeds from this book will be donated to the Bide-A-Wee Home Association. Bide-A-Wee is a not-for-profit charitable organization operating since 1903, consisting of shelters, clinics and memorial parks. Their humane work continues to help our animal friends in return for the pleasure they bring into our lives.

MESSAGE FROM THE AUTHOR

I have shared my life with dogs for as long as I can remember. As a baby, the first word I said was at the age of nine months. Much to the surprise of my parents, instead of the usual "mama" or "dada," my first word was "doggie." Dogs have always held a special place in my heart, and Boomerang was an extremely special dog. We were very closely bonded from the day he was born. I feel we were destined to be together for a greater mutual purpose, and our loving attachment is eternal.

As a first time author, I am firmly convinced that Boomerang channeled his thoughts and feelings through me in the creation of this book. The experience was intensely powerful and began a few days after his departure from the earthly plane. It was as if he was dictating and I was translating the impressions into words and placing them on paper. He clearly wished to share his special message with the entire world. I am truly honored that he chose me to be his messenger. Boomerang blessed me with his unconditional love, and he trusted me to relate his story exactly the way he would have wanted.

As he watches over me, I hope he is pleased with the outcome of this book, BOOMERANG - A MIRACLE. It seems even more miraculous that in reality he is the actual author, and I am merely the translator. I strongly suspect that Boomerang has always been an angel and always will be.

Arlene Millman

Boomerang — A Miracle Trilogy

BOOMERANG'S MESSAGE

Boomerang was a miraculous and wise teacher. I am thankful for the special time we shared together. Here is what I learned from my life with Boomerang:

** **B** e kind to others |||||
** **O** bserve nature's wonders
** **O** ptimism is contagious
** **M** iracles do happen
** **E** xpect the best
** **R** elate unselfishly
** **A** lways share joy
** **N** ever lose hope
** **G** ive love unconditionally
** **S** tay focused

** **M** ake others happy |||||
** **I** gnore the negative
** **R** efuse to give up
** **A** ccentuate the positive
** **C** hallenges create strength
** **L** ove can heal
** **E** veryday's a miracle!

I find it most helpful to make copies of this check-list, so it is available to review on a regular basis or whenever necessary.

BOOMERANG - A MIRACLE ENCORE

An Inspirational Tale for the New Millenium

by

Arlene Millman

Boomerang — A Miracle Trilogy

There are only two ways to live your life.
One is as though nothing is a miracle...
The other is as though everything is a miracle.

-- Albert Einstein

Miracles are of all sizes.
And if you start believing in little miracles,
You can work up to the bigger ones.

-- Norman Vincent Peale

Boomerang — A Miracle Trilogy

Boomerang — A Miracle Trilogy

CONTENTS

Boomerang — A Miracle Trilogy

DEDICATION

Dedicated to Boomerang and his miracle encore. May his story help all those who are searching for a miracle* and believe the possibility exists.

Love and kindness are intangibles, that cannot be destroyed by space or time. They are the indestructible building blocks of the universe. Through love, all things are possible.

*By definition, a miracle is any wonderful thing, fact or event. It appears to be neither a part of nor result of any known natural law.

ACKNOWLEDGMENTS

A special thank you to Mildred Engle, for being a devoted Boston Terrier breeder. She raised Boomerang with loving care during the first formative weeks of his return to Earth. Then she permitted me to "adopt" him, with her blessings, so that we could be together again. My sincere gratitude to Mildred for her kindness and cooperation.

A MIRACLE ENCORE

After spending some time in that place up above
He chose to return to the ones that he loved
It was indeed a miracle, an amazing surprise
To recognize his soul, by the look in his eyes.

My search was now over, my time was well spent
The perception was mutual, a miraculous event
Boomerang and I are united once more
What a wonderful blessing, a miracle encore!

He was truly an angel before his rebirth
Somehow he journeyed back, to a life here on Earth
What is his current mission, what does the future hold?
It will take awhile for the answers to unfold.

Together for a purpose, of this I am sure
Our unconditional love will always endure
Remembering the cosmic message, it is perfectly clear
Through love all things are possible, miracles do appear.

Boomerang — A Miracle Trilogy

PROLOGUE

The following is an inspirational tale for the new millenium.* It is a true story, based upon the miracle encore** of Boomerang.

This book is a sequel to BOOMERANG - A MIRACLE, a true story inspired by the original life of Boomerang. He lived on Earth for twenty-three short months, fulfilled his mission to spread unconditional love and joy-- then he became an angel.

Boomerang's tale now continues, as he chooses to return to Earth, reunites with his loved ones, and pursues his current mission for the new millenium.

His rebirth was indeed a miracle! And so, the amazing story of Boomerang's encore begins to unfold...

* Millenium describes a thousand year time span. Throughout this story "millenium" is spelled in a unique manner. The single N signifies a noteworthy ap-

proach to an established term.

** Encore is defined as an additional or re-peat performance. When used in context, it means again, once more.

PART 1

The RE-view

Millions of spiritual creatures walk the earth unseen, both when we sleep, and when we wake.

-- John Milton

Boomerang — A Miracle Trilogy

ONE

"An encore!" Boomerang exclaimed. "I can choose to have an encore," he repeated as his mind tried to grasp the full significance of the entire concept. It was complicated to comprehend and even more difficult to explain.

The prospect both intrigued and excited him. He had toyed with the idea frequently and tried to consider all the possibilities. It was a very tempting option. In simplistic terms, an encore meant he could return to Earth as a Boston Terrier once more, and be with the same family and friends again...just as before. His entire being tingled with a sense of elation and anticipation at the very thought. It was a wonderful opportunity! But, he also enjoyed the phenomenal benefits of being an angel. How could he decide what was the best choice for all concerned?

Grandpa Gem listened to Boomerang patiently, as always. He loved his grandson very much and wanted what was best for him. They were both full-fledged angels by now, but their relationship remained basically the same. Grandpa Gem was the indulgent grandfather, and Boomerang was his beloved and only grandson. He worshipped Grandpa Gem and still depended on him for wisdom and guidance. They were totally devoted to one another, and they always would be.

Meanwhile, Boomerang had an important decision to make, and he was torn in more than one direction. He thought back wistfully to all his loved ones still on Earth. He missed them terribly, and he knew the feeling was mutual.

Boomerang snuggled up to his grandpa. "How do I make the proper choice?" he mused as he contemplated his future.

"Be sure to reflect on all the possibilities, then look into your heart for the truth," Grandpa Gem replied with conviction. "Have faith you will make the correct choice when the time is right."

Boomerang's confidence was restored. As he dozed off that night, curled up next to Grandpa Gem, he decided to review his recent past in the pursuit of the answer.

TWO

Boomerang's transition to Heaven had been blissful. He took great delight in all the pleasures it offered, and he treasured his good fortune. Heaven was, to put it simply, perfectly heavenly. There were endless expanses of deliciously fragrant butterfly bushes, beautiful vistas blanketed with multi-hued flowers of assorted shapes and sizes, and perfectly symmetrical snowflakes glistening in the sunlight.

Heaven was a joyful place to be. Boomerang's entire being was filled with a sense of peace and happiness. He had access to all his favorite toys, especially Big Kahuna. Most important, he was with Grandpa Gem, whom he adored. They played and frolicked among the rainbows and butterflies. Everything radiated with an incandescent glow. It was charming and magical. Heaven was incredibly wonderful and euphoric!

In Heaven, Boomerang was unaffected by the limits of space and time. He was free to visit his loved ones back on Earth whenever he chose. He could see them and hear them, but he was unable to make direct physical contact. Of course they could not actually see or hear him, but he hoped his loving presence was felt to some degree. He visited often and reported back to Grandpa Gem with updates about their family and friends.

Mommy Crystal and Sister Penelope were still as beautiful as ever. His human mommy and daddy always looked wonderful in his eyes. However, he knew they missed him a great deal, and he could perceive their deep sorrow.

In fact, his human mommy was actually writing a book about him. He was both surprised and flattered, as he watched her preparing the manuscript. She was typing page after page, as she translated the notes she had written in a yellow spiral notebook. She seemed very intent and was concentrating so hard. He had never seen her so serious, as she leaned forward and poured over the notes in her lap. She wrinkled her brow and frequently sighed as she wiped the tears from her eyes with an already damp tissue.

Occasionally she would pause to look out the window at the sky above, before returning to the writing project. Boomerang knew she was thinking of him.

Can she feel me in the room with her at this very moment? Most likely. Just to be sure, he concentrated with every fiber of his being, and sent her all the unconditional love in his tremendously big heart.

Boomerang also visited his friends at the animal hospital on a regular basis, especially his favorite veterinarian, Dr. C. He loved Dr. C. and would always be grateful to him for prolonging the quality of his life on Earth. He would forever remember how Dr. C. had lovingly cared for him and treated him with extraordinary tendermess. Boomerang wished he could give Dr. C. a big kiss and tell him how much he admired and respected him.

How I wish everybody at the animal hospital could see me now, he fantasized. We would all be able to share hugs and kisses, just like before.

Of course his picture was still up on the bulletin board in the waiting room. It was in the very center of the bulletin board, and he watched people admiring him as they passed by.

I'm glad they find my picture attractive. But it's not quite the same as being there in person. How long has it been?

THREE

Boomerang was not certain how much time had elapsed since his arrival in Heaven. There were no seasons, as on Earth. No calendars or clocks were to be found, with which to mark the passing of time.

When it comes to space and time,

he reasoned, the contrast between Heaven and Earth is enormous.

Whenever he returned from a visit to the earthly plane, he became more aware of the extreme differences between the two places. He concluded they were probably located at opposite poles of the space-time continuum.

The pace in Heaven was leisurely, and the space was unstructured. Boomerang thought for a moment, and then he realized why...there is no time or space in Heaven. It was a difficult concept to explain, but it was not so complicated when experienced directly. Actually, it was all quite simple. Time was both instantaneous and perpetual; while space was vast and limitless. Therefore, there are no boundaries and no constraints, he surmised.

Most amazing of all, communication was silent, strong and true. Thoughts were transmitted via ultra-high-frequency energy patterns. Words were not necessary. Wordless communication occurred simultaneously, as thoughts and feelings were instantly exchanged and understood.

Boomerang often thought that those on Earth could use lessons in honest communication and understanding. He hoped that someday people would learn to share and show more compassion for each other, especially for those less fortunate.

Perhaps when I return to Earth on my next mission, I can be instrumental in teaching others the power of kindness. After all, he concluded, kindness is an essential link in the eternal cycle of life and love.

Boomerang fantasized often about returning to Earth, as he continued to reflect upon his decision.

FOUR

Meanwhile, back on Earth, events were proceeding at a rapid pace, in a parallel direction. Boomerang's human mommy and daddy missed him terribly, and thought about him constantly. His untimely departure had left a huge void in the entire household. Mommy Crystal and Sister

Boomerang — A Miracle Trilogy

Penelope also missed him very much. They kept hoping he would return so they could cuddle and play together again. It was just not the same without Boomerang. Everybody missed the hugs and kisses that were filled with his pure unconditional love.

Sometimes his human mommy thought she sensed his presence so strongly, she could almost reach out and touch him. She could feel him in the room with her, sending her wave after wave of unconditional love. One day she decided to write a book about Boomerang, as a loving tribute to his memory. He was indeed a miracle, and she wanted to share his story so that others might benefit.

Everyday, she spent hours sitting cross-legged on the family room floor, writing extensive notes in the spiral notebook on her lap. At night, she would sit at the keyboard to edit what she had written about Boomerang. This daily routine continued for many months. Whenever she needed additional inspiration, she would look out the window at the sky above, and she would visualize Boomerang up in Heaven.

When she needed to take a break from writing, she would walk outside and visit the colony of crows that resided in the yard. They were large birds, ranging in length from sixteen to twenty-one inches with rounded wings and tail. They were entirely black from their big bills to their legs and feet. She found the crows intriguing and enjoyed reading about their behavior and nesting habits.

When judged by human standards, crows were perhaps the most intelligent of all birds. They quickly learned new information and they could count, at least up through the single digits. They had a complex language and well developed social structure, including a sentry system. Crows were part of the Family Corvidae, which also contains the raven, rook and magpie. They were all closely related and referred to as corvids.

Although they were all covered

with glossy black feathers, each crow was unique in its appearance and personality. She had become quite attached to the colony of crows in the yard, and she gave them suitable nicknames, which they responded to. Junior was her favorite crow. She had saved his life several years ago when she found him lying prone on the grass in the backyard. He was unable to move, his breathing was labored and he was in obvious distress. Very gently she scooped him up, wrapped him in a towel and placed him in a large shoe box lined with newspapers. She drove to the animal hospital with the shoe box containing Junior on the seat beside her. She pleaded with them to save his life. They promised to try their best.

Junior was diagnosed with pneumonia. After three weeks of intensive care at the animal hospital, she was able to bring him home, nurse him back to health and release him back into the colony. She was told by the avian specialist that Junior was approximately six months old. Due to the respiratory illness, his growth would probably be stunted. But, otherwise, he was fully recovered and in good health. She was so relieved and thanked the specialist profusely.

As Junior grew up, he remained slightly smaller than the other crows, so he always looked younger and more juvenile--hence his name. He showed his appreciation in many ways. Everyday he entertained her with his amusing antics. At times, he serenaded her with his noisy banter, but she did not mind. She had grown very fond of Junior and appreciated all of his attributes.

Eventually, she became well acquainted with the rest of the colony. They all accepted her as an ally. There was Junior's friend Corbie, who had a cowlick in the middle of his back and was very philosophical by nature. Caw, who enjoyed a daily ritual of bathing regardless of the weather, was the acrobat and clown of the group. Finally, there was Sage the sentinel. He was the wisest and the oldest. His demeanor was large and imposing. The rest of the crow colony depended on him for protection, and they respected his judgment completely.

Sage's primary function, as sentinel, was to watch over the others and protect them from harm. He knew that the tallest location was the most ideal lookout. Sage would stand guard during daylight hours by positioning himself on the highest branch of an oak tree. He was more than sixty feet above the ground. This permitted him the best overall view of the area. When danger approached, he would utter a series of shrill cries and raucous screams to warn the others. Then he would soar down to the ground from his high perch to swiftly defend the area from the dangerous intruder.

At dusk, the crows would retire to their bulky nests, situated high among the foliage of the tall oak trees. The nests were large substantial baskets of sticks, stems, twigs and vines, lined with bark strips, earth, grass and moss. This afforded them snug protection during the evening hours from nocturnal predators, such as owls. It also shielded them from inclement weather, since the sturdy construction could withstand the rigors of rain, wind, snow and severe temperatures.

Boomerang's human mommy was kind and compassionate to all wildlife, but she had a particular soft spot in her heart for the crows. It was fascinating to watch the peculiar dynamics within their tightly knit hierarchy. She admired the crows for their loyalty to one another and enjoyed observing their gregarious behavior. They were inquisitive, full of mischief and could mimic the sounds of other animals.

According to ancient mythology, crows were considered to be the guardians of the cosmos. They were treated as sacred creatures, invested with special powers of perception. They were generally regarded as mysterious and mystical. She planned on gathering more background information and made a mental note to pursue additional research when time permitted. However, her first priority at the moment was to

Boomerang — A Miracle Trilogy

complete the manuscript about Boomerang.

PART 2

The RE-solution

Everything comes gradually and at its ap-
pointed hour.

-- Ovid

FIVE

While in Heaven, Boomerang and Grandpa Gem spent much of their leisure time together, just as they had on Earth. Boomerang considered it to be a real treat when Grandpa Gem would reminisce about "the good old days," as he referred to them. Boomerang particularly enjoyed hearing about when Grandpa Gem met Grandma Wendy, and how they had their only son, Daddy Burt. Eventually Daddy Burt met Mommy Crystal, which is how Sister Penelope came to be born. Within three years, Daddy Burt and Mommy Crystal had Boomerang, their only son and Grandpa Gem's only grandson. That was the concise version of Boomerang's family tree. His human mommy and daddy had called it a pedigree.

Boomerang also encouraged Grandpa Gem to share more traditional stories with him. He knew that traditions were the body of unwritten doctrines, customs and practices, handed down through successive generations.

If I can learn enough data about the past, he reasoned, I could apply it to the future. The more information I gather, the better equipped I will be for whatever circumstances might arise. "Knowledge is power," Grandpa Gem always said. Boomerang totally agreed.

One day Grandpa Gem asked Boomerang if he knew about the Legend of the Crows. Boomerang shook his head.

"According to an ancient folk legend," Grandpa Gem began, "crows are the messengers between Heaven and Earth. You could say they are an essential link in the cosmos," Grandpa Gem continued, "by keeping the channels of communication open and the transmission of vital knowledge flowing."

It took Boomerang some time to fully absorb everything Grandpa Gem had revealed about the Legend of the Crows.

"So if the legend is true," mused Boomerang, "they keep the information accurately circulating throughout the cosmos."

"A very wise deduction," praised Grandpa Gem. He marveled at his grandson's insight.

"If crows really are an indispensable link between Heaven and Earth, can they help with my decision?"

"No, unfortunately that's not possible. They can only assist after you have indicated your chosen path."

Grandpa Gem's response disappointed Boomerang, for the immediate answers still eluded him. Nevertheless, he still admired the crows for their legacy of wisdom. It was comforting to know he could rely on their help, after the decision was made.

"How will I know for sure whether I'm making the correct choice?"

As usual, when Boomerang had doubts, Grandpa Gem lovingly reassured him that all would be revealed in good time. Grandpa Gem reminded him that everything happens at the appropriate moment, if we are patient and allow the future to unfold naturally. Boomerang appreciated Grandpa Gem's words of wisdom. He felt at ease and he looked forward to the future with confident optimism.

SIX

Shortly thereafter everything happened in a most extraordinary and unforeseen way. Boomerang was summoned to a meeting of the highest ranking angels. It was rather unusual for a novice angel, such as himself, to be included in such a gathering. Much to his surprise, he was asked to be a part of the newly formed Angel Connection. The invitation was a great honor, and he accepted enthusiastically.

He was chosen for a pilot project, to help prepare the world for the new millenium. The new mission would be to teach those on Earth the unlimited power of unconditional love, and the miracle of universal kindness.

His immediate reaction was to think to himself, this will be a very challenging assignment. He pondered the enormous responsibility of this mission. A steady stream of images raced through his mind. What a unique opportunity! This is a very auspicious development. I have been chosen to function as an integral part of the Angel Connection, for the greater good of the world.

According to the information discussed at the meeting, it was Boomerang's understanding that with the approach of the new millenium, there was likely to be an increased level of awareness among the overall population. According to the theory, this raised collective consciousness on Earth meant people would be more receptive to new abstract concepts and more responsive to gestures of kindness.

The timing of the new millenium coincided perfectly with the cosmic expansion of the higher forces in Heaven. They were in complete alignment.

And so, the decision was finally determined. Boomerang would return to Earth, as one of the pioneers for the Angel

Connection. He resolved to proceed with the mission as quickly as circumstances permitted. All that remained was for him to determine the appropriate time and place, so the transition would be flawless.

Grandpa Gem highly approved of Boomerang's decision and commended him for making the correct choice. Grandpa Gem was bursting with pride. He also reminded Boomerang that he would be watching over him, and that their loving bond could not be broken by space or time. No matter where Boomerang went, as he pursued his current mission, Grandpa Gem would always be nearby. Boomerang felt completely certain that the future would be blessed. He was elated and began to make the necessary preparations.

Boomerang — A Miracle Trilogy

PART 3

The RE-turn

Time brings all things to pass.

-- Aeschylus

SEVEN

Boomerang bid Grandpa Gem a fond farewell before he departed for his mission back on Earth. The transition began slowly at first. Boomerang was calmly floating past endless clouds and rainbows. The views were astonishing...the colorful magnificence indescribable. Next thing he knew, he was soaring through space on his incredible journey back to Earth.

Dazzling colors swirled around him in an explosive display of beauty while the wind roared in the background. It was a miraculous phenomenon. Boomerang was filled with a sense of wonder. The entire experience had been awe inspiring! He was simultaneously excited and grateful.

This is just the beginning, thought Boomerang, as he prepared for his return to Earth. This is a wonderful new opportunity for me to accomplish important goals.

He arrived on a beautiful summer day in August. His birth was a joyous occasion for all concerned. He was a tiny black, brindle and white Boston Terrier, weighing in at eight ounces. He was even more beautiful than before. He had a pure white chest, a full white collar, and a heart radiant with love and kindness. And just as before, on the very top of his head was the definite shape of a boomerang. It was an unmistakable black outline on his pure white blaze, almost as if he had been stamped with indelible ink.

It was indeed a miracle, a miracle encore.

EIGHT

Boomerang was in a new, unfamiliar home, with a different family. He felt a little perplexed. So many questions swirled through his mind.

Where am I? And why do I have a new family? He was puzzled. Although confused by the circumstances, he knew the answers would be revealed at the appropriate time. More important, he remembered his mission as part of the Angel Connection on Earth.

He decided to focus on the sensory input of his brand new environment. Surrounded by a beautiful and loving Boston Terrier family, warmth and contentment filled his entire being. The immediate family consisted of Mommy Gigi (short for Gorgeous Girl), Daddy Talker and Sister Candi. Mommy Gigi was not just gorgeous, she was stunning! Daddy Talker was handsome in a rugged way, and he was very verbally inclined. He certainly lives up to his name, thought Boomerang. His new Sister Candi was cute as a button and sweet as could be. There was also his new human friend who took extra special care of him. She was kind and loving. Her name was Millie.

"You are the smartest most adorable puppy I've ever seen!" Millie would declare. Then she would kiss him repeatedly and tickle his tummy.

Boomerang loved all the attention he was receiving, and he felt very lucky to be part of such a wonderful household. He sent a loving message to Grandpa Gem, and remembered his words of wisdom extremely well. It was time to relax and enjoy the experience, while waiting patiently for the future to unfold.

Millie had been breeding Boston Terriers for many decades, and she immediately knew there was something exceptional about Boomerang. From the moment he was born, his behavior was very different from any of the other puppies she had raised. Although he played like a puppy, his overall demeanor seemed somehow older and more experienced. She marveled at his amazing self-sufficiency. During all her years of breeding, she had never seen anything like it.

Whenever she looked into his dark brown eyes, she sensed a high degree of knowledge, and the profound depth of his wisdom. It startled her and made her wonder.

Meanwhile, Boomerang's new life was indeed a miracle, a miracle encore! As the weeks passed, he grew big and strong.

Boomerang — A Miracle Trilogy

He had a sturdy body and a healthy constitution. He loved to play and enjoyed romping in the large fenced yard with his new Boston Terrier family--Mommy Gigi, Daddy Talker and Sister Candi.

His new human friend, Millie, fed him delicious meals, pampered him with the best of care, and took so many pictures of him. She said he was very photogenic, and she nicknamed him "Love Bug." One day, when he was a month old, she surprised him with a squeak toy in the shape of a butterfly. It was yellow latex with orange and blue stripes on its wings and two long green antennae.

How does she know I love butterflies? What a coincidence, he thought. The butterfly toy stirred memories deep within his heart and mind. He fondly recalled the details of his beautiful Black Knight butterfly bush back home. His human mommy and daddy had helped him to select it as a welcome home present after a prolonged stay at the animal hospital.

He had been so excited when they

planted the new butterfly bush in the garden. He adored butterflies. He took great delight in observing the colors and patterns on their wings, as they came fluttering into his yard. He would study their graceful movements for hours, mesmerized by their beauty.

Will I ever see my butterfly bush again? How I wish I could be there in the late spring when the deep purple flowers are beginning to bloom, he yearned. How I wish I could see my original family once again. Where could they be?

Although Boomerang was content with his new family and friend, he still longed for Mommy Crystal, Sister Penelope and most especially, his human mommy and daddy. He missed them terribly and hoped he would see them again soon.

Whenever Boomerang became too distracted by all the unresolved matters in his mind, he remembered Grandpa Gem's wise counsel. I must concentrate on my purpose, he vowed, and wait for the answers to appear.

Boomerang — A Miracle Trilogy

PART 4

The RE-cognition

Vision is the art of seeing things invisible.

-- Jonathan Swift

Boomerang — A Miracle Trilogy

NINE

The manuscript was finally complete.

Boomerang's human mommy had spent the past year totally immersed in writing about her beloved Boomerang.

With a sigh of satisfaction, she put the finishing touches on what she hoped would eventually become a published book. She let out another deep sigh and reflected upon the recent events of her life. Her devotion to Boomerang and his memory had initially inspired her to write this book about him.

People will read about the miracle of Boomerang, and they will also feel inspired, she thought. She hoped it would help people to believe in the possibility of miracles, and that through love, all things are possible.

While mulling over her hopeful expectation, she absently reached into the bottom desk drawer, searching for a large manila envelope. As she rummaged through the drawer, she noticed a folded piece of yellow paper that appeared to be torn from a legal size notepad. Across the top of the page, in bold red letters, were written the words: MILLIE'S MUTTS. Underneath the heading, there were two additional lines of red ink, listing a post office box and a telephone number. She peered at the scrawled characters and frowned.

She paused for a moment to think. Where did this come from? Who is Millie and where do I know her from? She tried to place the name, to remember where and when she had obtained it, but drew a complete blank. She couldn't imagine how the paper got in her desk. Perplexed, she set the yellow paper aside to deal with at another time.

She returned to the project at hand. At present, her prime focus was on the completed manuscript. She needed to visit the public library. Her plan was to diligently research which publishers would be most interested in her inspirational tale entitled, BOOMERANG - A MIRACLE.

But her mind kept wandering back to the yellow piece of paper with the red letters. She glanced once more at the page. It was an out of state address. The name MILLIE'S MUTTS did not provide a clue. She must have received it while at a dog show and filed it away for future reference, forgetting about it completely. She thought back to the last series of dog shows she had attended. They were with her beloved Champion Brandywine's Imperial Gem. She regularly accompanied Gem on the show circuit, throughout his long and successful career. But that was well over ten years ago.

She looked at the telephone number on the page. What were the chances that Millie's Mutts still had the same phone number? Highly unlikely. She made the call anyway. It was an unconscious decision, based on a strong intuitive sensation. A woman answered the phone on the third ring. And her name was Millie! Despite her surprise, she was most pleasant. Yes, she still lived at the same address, after all this time.

The remarkable concurrence of events were starting to feel like a miracle in the making. The conversation revealed that Millie had been breeding Boston Terriers for more than thirty years, and the latest litter of puppies was due shortly. Gorgeous Girl was the name of the expectant dam, and Talker was the sire. They further discussed their long time admiration of Boston Terriers, and their mutual interest in breeding and showing. Millie agreed that they most definitely had met at a dog show, but could not recall any of the particulars either.

"This is all so strange," Millie said. "Nevertheless, I'm so glad you called. It gave us an opportunity to become better acquainted. Please give me your phone number and mailing address so we can keep in touch."

Boomerang's human mommy complied, and she wished Millie good luck with the upcoming litter of puppies.

TEN

Less than a month later, Millie called to proudly announce that Gorgeous Girl (fondly known as Gigi) had delivered two beautiful, healthy Boston Terrier puppies--a boy and girl. She promised to send photographs soon. She just wanted to wait until their eyes were open, which usually occurs at about two weeks of age. Time passed...no photos arrived from Millie.

Boomerang's human mommy was so preoccupied with marketing her manuscript to an appropriate publisher, she forgot all about the puppies. Then one day in November, she received a priority package in the mail from Millie, the breeder she had met more than a decade ago, while attending a dog show with her beloved Gem.

She wiped a few stray tears from the corners of her eyes as she thought back wistfully to her first Boston Terrier champion. His finely chiseled features and regal bearing projected a strikingly handsome exterior image, while the gentle quality of his inner beauty radiated through with an unmistakable warmth and sweetness. Then she wiped even more tears from her eyes as she visualized his adorable grandson, Boomerang. She tried to ignore the intense longing in her heart. Perhaps someday she would see him once again, if it was part of the cosmic plan.

She was firmly convinced in the power of love to create miracles. Unconditional love will always endure, and miracles do happen to those who believe. Indeed, Boomerang had taught her that through love, all things are possible, even miracles. He had been a charming and wise teacher, and she was so very grateful.

Enough of this sentimental indulgence, she decided firmly. She reached for Millie's package and slit it open, curious to see what it contained. There were several Polaroid pictures, along with a handwritten letter. She scanned the letter briefly, then glanced through the photos.

Then it happened. In one of the photos there was an instantaneous sense of familiarity. Her head reeled and her heart skipped a beat, maybe more. Hope, surprise, doubt, disbelief -- the feelings blended together, creating a mixture of conflicting emotions. It was impossible to breathe, let alone think. Her stomach began to churn violently. She felt dizzy and light headed, as she stared at the photo still tightly grasped in her hand. She dared herself to peer at the photo more intently, and then tears began to stream down her face, blurring her vision. She refocused her eyes and took another look, just to make sure. It was Boomerang. She had recognized him immediately by the look in his eyes.

But how could this be? A little doubtful voice was chattering inside her head. Her ears began to ring. She felt her world tilt on its axis, and the surrounding room turned fuzzy, with the exception of the picture in her hand. How could this be, she repeated to herself over and over, the words drumming through her mind faster and faster. This is so incredible, she thought, trying to understand what was happening.

Then she began to laugh hysterically, followed by muffled sobs. Was she crying tears of joy or sorrow? She didn't honestly know. All that made sense to her now, all she really knew, was that she was looking at a picture bearing an uncanny resemblance to her beloved Boomerang. She was hoping beyond hope it was really him. She missed him so very much and thought about him constantly. Her heart ached with an all too familiar heaviness. There was a feeling of emptiness inside that nothing could fill, ever since Boomerang had departed from the earthly plane.

Her head was throbbing dully and her mind was swimming with unanswered questions. Could it really be? By some miracle, has he returned to me? Did she dare to dream of such a possibility? Would she really be reunited with her dear sweet Boomerang, after all this time? Was his physical presence really back on Earth and, if so, how and why?

She remembered the loving kisses

and cuddles he so generously bestowed upon family and friends. She remembered she had once decided to keep count and discovered that Boomerang shared over one thousand kisses during an average day! She thought about his strength of character and yet how gentle he was. One of Boomerang's favorite gestures was to place his paw ever so lightly on top of her hand, and then look directly into her eyes with love and devotion. She recalled looking back into the warmest deepest set of dark brown eyes she had ever seen. They seemed to connect directly with Boomerang's heart, and beam out rays of unconditional love that could comfort and heal in an instant. His eyes had a sheen that was inexplicably serene and tranquil. There were pinpoints of light that emanated from an unseen place deep within his soul. Boomerang's soul was so pure and his heart so full of love, his entire being was in total harmony with the universe.

Her heart was still heavy, but now there was a difference. There was a glimmer of light on the horizon, and she was hoping for a miracle. Regardless of the outcome, she would try to stay focused on the positive and finding out the truth. If Millie's puppy was indeed Boomerang, she would know him by the distinctive light in his eyes. She mentally prepared herself for all possibilities, but hoped for the best. If it's meant to be and the timing is right, she rationalized, then it will be my beloved Boomerang. And if not, then he's still on the heavenly plane with his Grandpa Gem. A few stray tears trickled down from the corners of her eyes, and she reached for the tissue box once again.

Then panic set in. If it is my Boomerang, and there is little doubt, I must call Millie immediately. What if she already promised him to somebody else? What if I'm too late? Anxious to speak with Millie, she dialed her number with trembling hands. Millie answered on the third ring. After the initial exchange of pleasantries, Boomerang's human mommy thanked Millie for sending the photos and inquired,

Boomerang — A Miracle Trilogy

"You know the handsome little male puppy, the one with the black outline on his pure white blaze? Well, uh, I was wondering...?" She trailed off, then finally blurted out, "Do you still have him, I mean, uh, is he available?"

"I sure do, and he's all yours, young lady!" was Millie's affectionate reply. "Something just told me he was waiting for you. I know dogs can't talk, but would you believe he sent me some sort of a message with those big beautiful brown eyes of his?"

Choking back tears, Boomerang's human mommy replied. "Yes, I would believe it. Indeed, his eyes are quite mesmerizing, even in the photo, and they are very familiar." Regaining her composure, she found the right words to explain the unusual set of circumstances to Millie, who was most gracious and understanding. They spoke at length and arranged for a visit the following weekend, and she began to make preparations for the upcoming trip.

The drive to Millie's house was

long and tiring. And yet, Boomerang's human mommy and daddy were so eager to see him again, they hardly noticed. The sun was setting when their car finally approached the gravel driveway in front of Millie's house. They walked up the front path and rang the doorbell. They both took a deep breath in anxious anticipation of this momentous and miraculous occasion.

PART 5

The RE-union

Reflect that life, like every other blessing,
derives its value from its use alone.

-- Samuel Johnson

144

ELEVEN

Boomerang was exactly three months old on the Saturday before Thanksgiving. It was late afternoon when the doorbell rang.

He ran into the front parlor to investigate the source. At that moment time stood still... and all dreams came true. His heart seemed to stop. In an instant he flew into the arms of his human mommy and daddy, showering both of them with hugs and kisses.

Boomerang was overcome with emotion. The reunion was simultaneously joyous and tearful. The event was a celebration of love. Their recognition had been immediate and mutual.

Boomerang's human mommy looked directly into his ever so familiar big brown eyes. She murmured, "We love you so much. Thank you for coming back to us."

Then she reached out for him, placed him in her lap and gently kissed the very top of his head where the black boomerang outline was clearly visible on his pure white blaze. She rhythmically stroked his soft fur and enjoyed the momentary feeling of serenity. He basked in the warmth of her love. She tenderly cradled him in her arms, while he snuggled comfortably against her body.

Millie had been observing the entire scene silently. She had watched the emotional reunion. Boomerang apparently shared a very strong bond with these people. She understood and wanted only the best for him. "He obviously belongs with the two of you," she offered. "He seems so content and happy, and he behaves as if he's been expecting you."

"I actually believe he has," Boomerang's human mommy responded.

After much discussion and extensive explanations, the details were finally worked out. It was decided they would spend the night at Millie's house and embark on their trip home the following day. At last, Boomerang would come home

146

again.

The next morning Boomerang enthusiastically hugged and kissed everybody good-bye. He felt relieved that his human friend, Millie, really understood. He was going back to where he belonged. He exchanged another round of hugs and kisses with Mommy Gigi, Sister Candi and Daddy Talker. They all agreed to visit each other often and made a pact to alternate visits whenever possible, due to the distance involved. He waved from the rear car window before settling in for the long ride home.

Boomerang was ecstatic! He was so blessed with good fortune. He had acquired a new extended Boston Terrier family, and Millie was a wonderful human friend. He was now reunited with his human mommy and daddy. By tonight he would be back home with Mommy Crystal and Sister Penelope.

He counted his blessings and was thankful to be part of the Angel Connection on Earth. Boomerang was so happy, and he knew that Grandpa Gem was contentedly watching over him with a deep sense of satisfaction and pride. It was indeed a miracle, a miracle encore!

TWELVE

The first few weeks back home were quite hectic for Boomerang. There were so many things to do and people to see. He needed to catch up on everything that had happened while he was away.

He made several trips with his human mommy to the animal hospital. He wanted to visit all his friends there, and especially his favorite veterinarian, Dr. C.

When Dr. C. saw Boomerang, he recognized him immediately and exclaimed, "Boomerang, you look fantastic! It's so terrific to see you again."

With that, Boomerang gave Dr. C. dozens of wet kisses on his nose, cheeks, ears and neck. He wanted to let Dr. C. know how happy he was to be back.

Dr. C. also examined Boomerang

thoroughly and gave him a clean bill of health. "He weighs almost twelve pounds and he looks great. He is in excellent health and there is no need to be concerned this time."

His human mommy, who had been cautiously optimistic, was relieved and thanked Dr. C. for his dedication to Boomerang.

On the way out, she left a new picture with the receptionist to be placed on the bulletin board in the waiting room. His previous picture was still in place on the bulletin board, as well, which flattered Boomerang tremendously.

Since it was almost the holiday season, his human mommy and daddy thought it would be fun to visit Santa Claus and his reindeer. They took several photos of Boomerang with Santa, so there would be extra copies for his friend Millie.

He especially enjoyed posing for pictures with the reindeer. He wore a pair of fuzzy imitation antlers on his head, so they would all match. He looked like a cute little black and white reindeer.

He was filled with so much merriment and mirth. In the spirit of sharing, Boomerang wanted to surprise Millie with a holiday gift package, containing photos for her, and some special toys for his Boston Terrier family.

So, after the photo session, Boomerang joined his human mommy and daddy for a shopping expedition at the local pet boutique. They helped him to select a variety of toys for both his Boston Terrier families. It gave Boomerang great pleasure to share with others. By giving, he received the greatest joy. His human mommy and daddy asked him to choose whatever he desired for himself. They loved him so much and were so grateful to have him back. They wanted to shower him with presents.

Boomerang graciously declined. I have the best present in the whole world, he thought. I am surrounded by the ones that I love. Besides, he already possessed everything he wanted. He had all the toys he could ever wish for—especially his favorite Big Kahuna and the new yellow butterfly from Millie. His previous wardrobe still fit him perfectly. He particularly favored his red turtleneck sweater with the blue, yellow and green swirls. His patent leather Sherpa bag, with the leopard trim and plush lambskin interior, was almost brand new and still suited him well. Nobody else had used it while he had been away. It was his favorite mode of transportation, and provided a cozy, safe environment for traveling in the car.

The more he thought about it, the more Boomerang realized there was nothing else he really needed or wanted. He had been back on Earth just a little over four months, and he was totally content. He knew that happiness did not depend on how much you had to enjoy, but how much you enjoyed what you had. In his infinite wisdom, Boomerang had discovered the ultimate secret of happiness.

Boomerang — A Miracle Trilogy

PART 6

The RE-velation

No act of kindness, no matter how small, is
ever wasted.

--Aesop

THIRTEEN

Eventually Boomerang settled into a comfortable routine. It felt as if he had never left. He appreciated his life and counted his blessings daily. He was happy, healthy and surrounded by enormous amounts of unconditional love, which he always enjoyed returning with interest. Boomerang always tried to be kind, considerate and concerned about others. This was his natural way of being, and he was committed to providing a constant example of unconditional love to others. He was anxious to concentrate on his current mission, and ready to put his energy to good use. Boomerang was focused on his goal and felt a huge responsibility as a part of the Angel Connection.

The weather had been unseasonably warm for the time of year. In fact, the temperature had reached record highs into the mid-seventies, throughout the month of December. The trend seemed to be continuing well into January. Boomerang thought it was great. Something to do with El Niño, he had heard.

The unusually mild winter weather afforded him the opportunity of spending an extensive amount of time outdoors, communing with nature. He had always appreciated the wonders of nature and he still marveled at the beauty of a rainbow, the symmetry of a snowflake and the graceful formation of birds in flight. He was always amused by the rabbits romping across the grass, the bushy-tailed squirrels playing tag in the trees, and the chipmunks scurrying through the garden gathering food in preparation for their hibernation season.

The Black Knight butterfly bush was the best treat of all. Boomerang calculated his butterfly bush must be almost two years old, and it had more than doubled in size. Was he ever surprised!

He loved to gaze at it, and to remember the day he first saw the beautiful bush at the local garden nursery. Of course, the huge clusters of deep purple flowers would not bloom again until next spring, but Boomerang thought the bush still looked beautiful with its long slender branches reaching up to the sky. He looked forward to springtime when the brightly colored tubular shaped flowers produced their nectar. The strong fragrance of the nectar would then attract a plentiful supply of his favorite butterflies in all the colors of the rainbow. Boomerang was so happy! He would be able to watch his butterfly bush grow for many years to come.

This time he was strong and healthy with an important long-term mission to fulfill. This time his presence would be needed on Earth well into the new millennium. Boomerang was an important link of the Angel Connection. As such, his current mission was to help teach others the power of unconditional love and kindness.

I know the extraordinary power of love and kindness from first-hand experience, he thought. The question is, how do I best share this knowledge with the rest of the Earth's population? He pondered his dilemma, hoping for a spark of inspiration.

FOURTEEN

Assistance came a short while later from a totally unexpected source. Boomerang was outside in the yard enjoying an unusually warm and sunny winter day. Surprisingly, Mommy Crystal and Sister Penelope had chosen to remain indoors for their afternoon nap.

This was an opportunity for Boomerang to become better acquainted with the colony of crows residing in the area. He had spent quite some time recently, observing them on his own. Their behavior was truly fascinating. Grandpa Gem had also briefed him on specific details and background information that might be useful someday.

Several years ago, Boomerang's human mommy had saved a young crow's life. His name was Junior, as he was the smallest member of the crow colony at the time. She had been so kind and caring to

Junior, that the entire crow community was eternally grateful. She was goodhearted and compassionate, and they loved her for it. She had become their friend. In return, they were concerned about her welfare and available to help whenever necessary.

From Grandpa Gem's description, Boomerang was easily able to identify the crows by name. Junior was slightly smaller than the rest and the most gregarious. Junior's friend, Corbie, had a cowlick on his back and he was the most philosophical. Caw enjoyed a daily bath regardless of the weather, and was a natural acrobat. The oldest and wisest crow of the colony was Sage the sentinel. He was logical and practical. His primary responsibility was to watch over and protect the others. The crows functioned well as a team. They seemed to be in perfect harmony with each other and the universe.

He had been quietly observing the crows from a distance when Junior flew over and landed on the branch of an oak tree nearby. Silhouetted against the bright blue winter sky, his lustrous black feathers reflected the sunlight, and his dark eyes glinted with flecks of gold. His outstretched wings cast a diagonal shadow on the lawn, directly across from where Boomerang stood.

Boomerang looked up and nodded to Junior. "Hello," he said. "Thank you for coming over to visit. I was hoping we could become better acquainted." He smiled shyly and waited for a friendly reply.

"Welcome home," responded Junior. "It's good to have you back. That was quite a long car ride from Millie's house." Then he sat back and gave a deep chuckle.

Boomerang was stunned. "How did you know that?" he gasped.

"We were involved in the entire process," Junior revealed. "In fact, we were instrumental in helping your human mommy locate you," he confessed as he glided effortlessly down to the ground, landing just a few feet from Boomerang.

"That's absolutely amazing! Do you

Boomerang — A Miracle Trilogy

have supernatural powers? Is the Legend of the Crows really true?" The questions came tumbling out so quickly, Boomerang could hardly catch his breath.

Junior moved even closer as he proceeded to elaborate. "Let's just say we possess an expanded level of consciousness, due to a higher vibrational frequency. Our awareness of the cosmos is vast; we see thoughts as energy in its purest form."

Boomerang was mesmerized. He encouraged Junior to please continue his discourse.

"Crows are the traditional messengers between Heaven and Earth," he said with pride. "Our responsibilities include protection and assistance. We are also the guardians of the portals between Heaven and Earth. Our purpose is to prevent unsavory elements from passing through undetected. We grant permission and give clearance only when it is worthwhile and for the greater good." Junior paused for a moment before continuing. "Crow spelled backwards is worc--which sounds like work," he quipped, "and we take our work very seriously." He gave Boomerang a playful wink.

Boomerang winked back and said, "How ingenious." He was really impressed with Junior's high degree of intelligence and keen sense of humor.

They continued to converse at length, becoming fast friends in the process. Boomerang explained his current mission in greater detail, and Junior offered to assist him. They exchanged relevant information and speculated about the turn-of-the-millenium experience.

Junior revealed that the new millenium would be heralded in by a major shift of the Earth's spiritual energy, followed by a dynamic manifestation of creative forces throughout the cosmos. He also revealed there would be subtle changes on the spirit level, affecting the scope of human faith and belief values.

Boomerang had been listening intently. "How we are at present and where we will be in the future are of great concern to me," he confided.

"As they should be," agreed Junior. He could be every succinct when time was a factor. With dusk approaching, it was essential for him to depart quickly.

They made plans to meet again the following day. Meanwhile, Boomerang tried to digest everything Junior had told him thus far. It was all so amazing. It was indeed a miracle...a mega-miracle of the new millenium!

- FIFTEEN

The next morning, Junior arrived with his friend Corbie. He introduced Boomerang to Corbie, explaining that Corbie had asked to join them. He wanted to be of assistance, and he had a pertinent suggestion.

Boomerang then reiterated that his purpose--his reason for being--was to teach others the power of unconditional love and the miracle of kindness. This was his current mission, as part of the Angel Connec-

163

tion on Earth.

"We would like to help you form a Kindness Network," Junior said simply. "According to Corbie, a single act of kindness is contagious. Whoever is on the receiving end of an act of kindness will be appreciative and naturally want to pass it on."

"That's correct," chimed in Corbie. He was anxious to explain the basis of his philosophy. Corbie proceeded to reveal his conclusions. "Kindness is contagious," he began methodically, "because each act of kindness begets another. Someone on the receiving end of a kind gesture will send another kindness back out, as individuals are linked together by the inherent inertia of the process." He took a deep breath, encouraged by the fact that both Boomerang and Junior were nodding their approval. "As the cycle continues, the acts of kindness will spiral outward, expanding in ever-widening circles throughout the Earth. There is no limit to the extent of the expansion. Eventually, the Kindness Network can expand cohesively, to touch every being on Earth--human and animal alike."

After some reflection, Junior said, "I think Corbie's suggestion makes a great deal of sense. It has merit and deserves serious consideration. Keep in mind," he added, "a single act of kindness need not be complicated. It can be as simple as a smile. A smile is priceless. It can change attitudes and bring happiness. Yet, it costs nothing to give."

Boomerang had been quietly listening, trying to absorb all the details of Corbie's philosophy. He felt the excitement building and could no longer contain his emotions. "The whole concept is phenomenal, Corbie. You are brilliant. Let's do it!" He was more than pleased with Corbie's suggestion; he was overjoyed. After he was able to regain his composure, he thanked both Corbie and Junior profusely for their kind assistance.

And so it was unanimously decided. They were officially forming a Kindness Network.

Boomerang's mission was under-way.

SIXTEEN

Boomerang had gained tremendous insight from his meeting with the crows. He briefly summarized in his mind what they had discussed, regarding the formation of a Kindness Network.

Random acts of kindness have the power to link individuals together by virtue of their inherent inertia and cohesion. One simple act of kindness can multiply and eventually expand to touch many lives. By the new millenium, there are likely to be numerous mini-miracles happening throughout the world as the result of the Kindness Network. These mini-miracles, in turn, will cohesively link up to create the mega-miracles of the new millenium. It would become an automatic process, unlimited in scope, originating from the forces of love and kindness.

Boomerang knew that uncondi-

Boomerang — A Miracle Trilogy

tional love manifests as dynamic spiritual energy, which can create miracles. His return to Earth and reunion with his loved ones were solid proof that through love, all things were possible, especially miracles.

He felt inspired by the expanded responsibilities of his current mission, and he was proud to be an essential part of the Angel Connection. With the approach of the new millenium, there would be a shift in consciousness. He anticipated a rapid increase in the spiritual awareness of the Earth's population. The timing was perfect. He was on the bridge to the 21st century, and he was prepared for whatever challenges he might encounter.

This was a whole new beginning for Boomerang, coinciding with a whole new millenium for the world.

THE END

EPILOGUE

Opinions differ as to when the new millenium is officially scheduled to start. Some insist it starts as of January 1, 2000. Others say it will begin the following year. According to accurate sources, the new millenium actually begins on January 1, 2001. (From January 1 to December 31, 2000 is the year preceding the new millenium.)

Regardless of which version you agree with, one thing is certain. The new millenium is the perfect time to join the Kindness Network. Please help Boomerang with his current mission. Each act of kindness begets another. Until, like ripples in a pond, the concentric circles begin to touch one another. In the spirit of the Kindness Network, a portion of the proceeds from this book will be donated to needy humans and animals through appropriate not-for-profit charitable organizations.

Kindness is doing something meaningful for one who really needs it. Kindness is the quality of being goodhearted and considerate, unselfish and caring. Kindness is contagious. Kindness is indeed a miracle!

Boomerang — A Miracle Trilogy

MESSAGE FROM THE AUTHOR

In searching for the truth, I found Boomerang once again. By trying to help others, I received unconditional love in return.

As with my previous book, BOOMERANG - A MIRACLE, I am firmly convinced that Boomerang channeled his thoughts and feelings through me in the creation of this sequel. It really was a collaborative effort. The portions that were not channeled, are based on actual events in our lives.

I am truly honored that he chose to return to me once again. He has blessed me with unconditional love for the second time. It is indeed a miracle, a miracle encore.

Arlene Millman

Boomerang — A Miracle Trilogy

BOOMERANG'S MESSAGE

Boomerang's encore is indeed a miracle! I am extremely thankful for the additional time we are sharing together. He is a wise and patient teacher. Here is what I have learned from living with Boomerang:

** **B** e kind to others

** **O** bserve nature's wonders

** **O** ptimism is contagious

** **M** iracles do happen

** **E** xpect the best

** **R** elate unselfishly

** **A** lways share joy

** **N** ever lose hope

** **G** ive love unconditionally

** **S** tay focused

** **E** xtend a helping hand

** **N** ever give up

** **C** reate miracles through love

** **O** pen your heart

** **R** each for your goals

** **E** xperience life fully!

I find it most helpful to make copies of this check-list, so it is available to review on a regular basis or whenever necessary.

BOOMERANG
- A MIRACLE ODYSSEY

An Inspirational Journey

by

Arlene Millman

To me every hour of the light and dark is a miracle. Every cubic inch of space is a miracle.

--Walt Whitman

Boomerang — A Miracle Trilogy

CONTENTS

Dedication
Acknowledgements
Poem
Prologue

Epilogue

Message from the Author

Boomerang's Message

Appendix

DEDICATION

On with the dance! Let joy be un-
confined.

-- Lord Byron

Dedicated to my beloved Boomerang, who has been a constant source of
unlimited joy and inspiration.

May his continuing story help
spread unconditional love and kindness
throughout the world--especially to those
who are searching for a miracle.

ACKNOWLEDGMENTS

A big thank you to Joann Hampar for her guidance. She encouraged me to share the experience, and write about the miracle of Boomerang, so that others might benefit.

A MIRACLE ODYSSEY

He awoke to the news, an upcoming vacation
To a rugged land, at a distant location
Preparations were made, he was eager to go
There was so much to see, a magnificent show.

Expect some surprises, Boomerang had been told
An exciting journey is about to unfold
In the red rock country, his soul found the key
It was indeed, a miracle odyssey!

His spirits soared higher than ever before
While enjoying the vistas and local lore
The future presented a powerful view
Of unlimited choices, to begin anew.

The third millenium was approaching fast
A time to go forward and learn from the past
Boomerang's purpose, his mission from above
Spreading kindness, while teaching the power of love.

Boomerang — A Miracle Trilogy

PROLOGUE

The following is an inspirational journey into the portals of the 21st century. It is an odyssey* based upon the life of Boomerang.

This book is the third in a series. The original tale, BOOMERANG - A MIRACLE, was a true story inspired by the miraculous** life of Boomerang. He was a tiny little dog, with a tremendously big heart and a mission to fulfill. He lived on Earth for twenty-three short months, fulfilled his mission to spread unconditional love and joy -- then he became an angel.

In the sequel, BOOMERANG - A MIRACLE ENCORE, he chooses to return to Earth as an integral part of the Angel Connection, reunites with his loved ones, and pursues his mission for the new millennium -- to teach people the power of unconditional love and the miracle of kindness. His rebirth was indeed a miracle!

Boomerang's tale now continues, as he embarks on an inspirational journey and faces the challenges of the 21st century. He approaches his current mission with exceptional wisdom, unbridled joy, and unconditional love. And so, the amazing story of Boomerang's odyssey begins to unfold....

* Odyssey describes a long, wandering journey, involving travel from one place to another.

** Miraculous is synonymous with wonderful or amazing. It is defined as anything which is so marvelous or extraordinary that it is usually attributed to, or apparently caused by, the direct intervention of a supernatural power.

Part 1

The View

The best thing about the future, is
that it comes one day at a time.

-- Dean Acheson

ONE

The view was panoramic. The view was an incredibly spectacular display of shapes and colors, extending in every direction. It was a kaleidoscope of swirling images, flowing from an invisible source. The images oscillated, and then blended together, forming a seamless landscape. It stretched from a timeless past... to a future of endless possibilities. The view was all encompassing and infinite, reflecting exquisite messages of harmony and beauty. It was both anything and everything one could ever imagine. The magnitude was one of eternal expansion, surrounded by images of darkness and light. There were mirror-like reflections of universal vistas, both turbulent and serene. The enhanced colors shimmered and danced on waves of light that serpentined in coiled, circular random patterns, while the smoky shadows receded into the background.

The intensity of the landscape design was too vivid for him to fully comprehend. The view defied description. It could be experienced and appreciated he thought, but it would be nearly impossible to explain or measure. In many ways, it's quite similar to Heaven, he mused. Mesmerized by the intricate beauty, Boomerang sat back and absorbed the unobstructed view, wishing Grandpa Gem were there to share the experience with him.

Boomerang continued to enjoy the view from the bridge for awhile longer. I must remember to try telling Grandpa Gem my impressions of the view the next time I visit him in Heaven. Perhaps he can arrange to meet me at the bridge so we can watch the heavenly view together. Boomerang missed his grandpa a great deal, and he always looked forward to their visits with eager anticipation. I hope Grandpa Gem will be as enthusiastic about the view as I am. His entire being quivered with excitement at the very thought. Boomerang loved his Grandpa Gem very much and tried to please him whenever possible. This would be a perfect opportunity.

Boomerang — A Miracle Trilogy

Boomerang turned his full attention back to the view from the bridge. The bridge provided a transformational link from present-day life to encounters with the future. He was on the bridge to the 21st century. This is where he came whenever he needed to contemplate the past, or scan the horizon of the future. The bridge offered a view that was both clear and pure, affording a fresh perspective. As he looked toward the hopes of the future, Boomerang was bathed in golden sunlight. When he gazed at the view, his optimism knew no bounds. The new millenium was rapidly approaching. So far, it was free of imperfections and filled with infinite possibilities and endless dreams.

The countdown was underway. Preparations were in full swing throughout the Earth to herald in the third millenium. Celebrations were being planned and journeys scheduled. Everybody wanted to be someplace memorable when the new millenium finally arrived. The air was crackling with excitement as more and more festivities were anticipated to mark the inception of a new era.

There was also increasing speculation regarding the future of the world as we now know it. The media publicity emphasized certain suggested preparations, in case of computer malfunctions and widespread communication breakdowns. Boomerang had heard people refer to the Y2K dilemma very often, voicing concerns related to disruptions in banking, and difficulties in obtaining food and other necessary supplies. There was also a great deal of publicity and conjecture focused on travel arrangements, cautioning people to avoid scheduling flights during the transition from New Year's Eve (12/31/99) to New Year's Day (01/01/00). This was supposedly a precaution, just in case the Y2K bug caused computers to malfunction while an airplane was enroute, and the tower was unable to contact the flight crew, to prepare for landing.

Boomerang thought long and hard about these issues. However, he was not alarmed. While the Earth's population was primarily concerned with these mundane matters, he was concentrating on the over-view from the bridge. His insight was vi-sionary. His wisdom a cumulative result of all his previous Earthly missions. It was all so clear.

There were actually two new mille-nium dates -- depending on one's frame of reference. The new technological mille-nium would begin at the stroke of midnight on 01/01/00. That was because the calen-dars, clocks, computers and other measur-ing devices needed to be re-programed. The standard two-digit prefix, for the dura-tion of the 20th century and throughout the second millenium, always began with the number one, culminating with the number nineteen for the past century. The third millenium necessitated a two-digit prefix beginning with the number two, and the constant prefix for the upcoming 21st cen-tury would be the number twenty. Due to inefficient planning and lack of sufficient foresight, the necessary modifications had been overlooked completely or were incomplete in many instances. That is what all the confusion and commotion was about.

Meanwhile, in his infinite wisdom, Boomerang knew that the new millenium would not actually begin until 01/01/01. The time span between 01/01/00 and 12/31/00 was the highly significant premillenial year. This was a time of serious spiritual preparation, when those on Earth would experience a gradual subliminal change of consciousness, followed by a rapid new awareness of the metaphysical dimensions. These expanded levels of awareness would result in better communications and deeper mutual understanding.

Boomerang was quite pleased with this projection for the Earth's population. And so, while the masses were concentrating on the technological millenium, he was immersed in preparations for the spiritual millenium. As an integral part of the Angel Connection on Earth, this was his cosmic responsibility.

Boomerang — A Miracle Trilogy

As he surveyed the view from the bridge, Boomerang thought about his current mission. There was so much to accomplish, for he had been entrusted with a mighty task. He knew there would be many challenges to face, but he was prepared. As an essential member of the Angel Connection, Boomerang had chosen his return to Earth -- to teach people the power of unconditional love and the miracle of kindness.

The future prospects of the Kindness Network were most promising. The goal was to help spread kindness throughout the Earth's population, in ever-expanding concentric circles. Kindness is contagious. Therefore, as each act of kindness begets another, the circles start to touch one another, forming an interlacing network. Eventually, the Kindness Network would begin to multiply in great numbers, according to a previously determined, carefully calculated, exponential formula.

Kindness is indeed a miracle,

thought Boomerang. An important part of my mission is to teach people the miracle of kindness. With the expanded level of consciousness, minds and hearts will be more receptive, he mused, so the Kindness Network will build up speed and momentum as never before. Boomerang felt confident that within a short while, the Kindness Network would be influencing the population in both hemispheres and around the globe.

TWO

Suddenly, Boomerang was jolted awake by the insistent ringing of the telephone. He had been in a deep slumber, snuggling between Sister Penelope and Mommy Crystal. A patch of early morning sunlight filtered through the window, highlighting tawny flecks of brindle on his primarily black coat. He stretched and rolled onto his back, enjoying the penetrating warmth of the mid-winter sun.

It was February, the sky was a

Boomerang — A Miracle Trilogy

bright blue, and the day promised to be beautifully crisp and clear. The temperatures had been unseasonably moderate for the northeast region, and that suited Boomerang just fine. He hoped the remainder of the winter would continue to stay mild, due to the supposed influence of El Niño or La Niña -- he wasn't sure which one the meteorologists had agreed upon. Either way, he preferred warmer weather, as it afforded him a greater opportunity to spend time outdoors with the crows, especially Junior. They had become quite close, since Boomerang returned home last fall, and they could spend hours enjoying each other's company. Together, they exchanged information, planned for the new millenium, and discussed the expansion of the Kindness Network.

Junior crow was assisting Boomerang with his current mission -- to teach people the power of unconditional love and the miracle of kindness -- and Boomerang had come to rely heavily on his help and guidance. Sometimes, Junior's friend, Corbie the philosophical crow, would join in their conversations. He, too, offered Boomerang wise counsel. Meanwhile, Sage the sentinel crow would remain high up in the treetops, offering his support and protection. Caw, the acrobatic crow, also visited with Boomerang on a regular basis. He behaved in a zany manner, and he could mimic to perfection. Caw would take his daily bath, a ritual he adhered to regardless of the weather, and then fly off to dry. His visits were quick and entertaining, providing an interval of comic relief whenever necessary.

On this particular morning, Boomerang knew it was a special day. He cocked his head on an angle, and pricked his upright ears in the direction of his human mommy's voice. He could hear her speaking on the telephone. It became apparent that she was talking to Millie, Boomerang's best human friend.

Millie was a devoted Boston Terrier breeder. She had raised him with loving care during the first formative weeks of his new life. Then she permitted his human mommy to "adopt" him with her blessings, so they could be together once again. Millie was kind and caring, and she loved him very much.

As he listened to the conversation, Boomerang realized that today was Millie's birthday. He was delighted! How exciting, he thought. Boomerang had taken great pleasure in helping his human mommy choose the perfect gift for Millie. She had been breeding Boston Terriers for over thirty years, and her house contained an extensive collection of Boston Terrier memorabilia. She had standing and sitting figures, made of porcelain, wood, brass, pewter and glass. There were pictures, plates. pillows, plaques and paperweights. There was an array of large and small trophies, ribbons, glassware, lamps, books and statues. However, there was one item Millie did not yet possess.

Boomerang and his human mommy found the perfect birthday gift in a local antique shop. Off in the corner there was a beautiful large tapestry, draped across the back of a wooden rocking chair. The fabric was soft and lustrous, and there was a thick row of fringe on all four sides. The tapestry scene depicted groups of Boston Terriers, posing and playing in a Victorian garden setting. In the background were lush flowers and graceful trellises, adorning a sprawling lawn. Boomerang knew instantly that Millie would love it. He was so happy and excited to be able to share his discovery with her!

His human mommy purchased the tapestry, packed it carefully, and shipped it in plenty of time to arrive by her birthday. She also enclosed a birthday card that they had all signed -- his human mommy and daddy, Sister Penelope, Mommy Crystal, and of course, Boomerang. It had been great fun to dip his front paws into the red vegetable dye, and then press them onto the paper. The card was covered with paw prints and filled with much love.

"Yes, Millie," he heard his human mommy say, "we'll definitely see you soon. I'll be certain to tell Boomerang you called and give him a big kiss from you. He'll be absolutely thrilled you're so pleased with the gift! He helped me to select it, you know. In fact, he noticed it the moment we walked into the store."

Then he heard his human mommy say something about an upcoming trip to the red rock country.

"Please let us know when you plan on going, so we can try to coordinate the dates. I'm sure Boomerang would be most interested in meeting Angel."

Who is Angel? Am I in for some sort of surprise? He adored surprises, and his curiosity shifted into high gear. He continued to listen, but their conversation was finally winding down.

"Have a wonderful birthday, Millie, and enjoy the tapestry...By the way, how are Mommy Gigi, Sister Candi and Daddy Talker?"

She paused a moment as she waited for Millie's reply.

"That's great! I'm so glad. Please

give everybody our love. I'll be calling you the next time. Bye now."

Boomerang pondered over the conversation. He thought Angel was an unusually beautiful name. How is it connected to Millie, he wondered. And the repeated references to a place called the red rock country. What was that? Where was his human mommy planning on taking him? His curiosity was beginning to peak again.

Questions swirled through his mind, but the answers eluded him.

Would Junior know the answers? Most likely. Boomerang made a mental note to ask him when time permitted. Junior was omniscient -- he possessed infinite knowledge of all things. Crows were all empowered with the basic gift of universal omniscience. However, they were only permitted to reveal what was really necessary, at the appropriate time, and when there was a sufficient need to know.

Boomerang — A Miracle Trilogy

THREE

Lately Boomerang's human mommy had been spending a great deal of her time on the telephone. Most of her calls were to publishers and agents. She was looking for the appropriate venue to publish her book, entitled BOOMERANG - A MIRACLE. It was inspired by Boomerang's previous life on Earth, and she was determined to locate a publisher who would appreciate the true tale and promote it with heartfelt enthusiasm.

However, since the conversation with Millie on her birthday, she was involved with a great many travel related calls. At first she was calling airlines. Boomerang heard her ask about schedules, onboard pet regulations and seat selections.

"Will he be needing a health certificate for interstate travel?" she asked.

She was holding the cordless phone in one hand while she rapidly took notes with the other. The lined memo pad on the table served to organize her thoughts.

"I see," she said, then asked, "How long is it good for?"

Her last few questions related to his Sherpa bag, which had always been his favorite mode of transportation in the car. She crossed her fingers and continued. "Is a Sherpa bag permissible for onboard airline travel? What are the acceptable dimensions that will fit under a seat in the cabin? Will you allow us to reserve a bulkhead row? Yes, that would be perfect! Thank you, you've been very kind."

She smiled and seemed pleased with all the answers. It was smooth sailing so far.

"Well, Boomerang, we're making great progress. We have all our flights arranged. Now, for the room accommodations."

Boomerang was happily curled up by her side. After giving him several hugs and kisses, she began to call hotels. He listened intently, eager to hear more.

"Can you please tell me if you accept small pets?" she would ask. "Are there any restricted areas where pets are not permitted on your property? What about the swimming pool and adjacent patio?"

With each successive phone call, she continued to jot down detailed notes until the entire memo page was filled with columns of relevant information and comparative data. Finally she seemed satisfied with the results of her research. Her attention to details had paid off. During the course of one afternoon, after reviewing her extensive notes, she decided to order the airline tickets and reserve the hotel accommodations. She also arranged for a limousine to take them to the airport. When they arrived at their destination, a rental car would be waiting. The arrangements were complete. Everything had flowed smoothly without obstacles, she thought. That was an auspicious sign of things to come. With a deep sense of satisfaction, she proceeded to review her trip check-list of things to do before departure.

Boomerang was getting really excited! He was actually going on a vacation with his human mommy and daddy. Sister Penelope and Mommy Crystal had chosen to stay home. It was their preference. Since they were not the best of travelers, they preferred the familiarity of their house to the adventure of an unknown destination. Boomerang respected their decision, and friends would be staying with them while he was away. He would miss them, but he knew they would be well cared for.

In the evenings, his human mommy and daddy would read the many glossy travel brochures that had arrived in the mail. They planned their itinerary and discussed the pros and cons of guided tours versus independent exploration. They added to their list of sightseeing options, talking about: jeep tours, balloon adventures, canyon lands, volcanic rims, waterfalls, petroglyphs and medicine wheels. And then they mentioned that term again that he had heard several weeks before -- red rock country. I must ask Grandpa Gem for an explanation, he vowed.

Boomerang — A Miracle Trilogy

They were planning a fantastic journey, and best of all, he was included! There were still so many preparations and plans to finalize. There was last minute shopping and, of course, packing.

Boomerang's human mommy and daddy took him on a shopping expedition to his favorite pet boutique. He had been there frequently, both during this lifetime and his prior life. It was where he had chosen his black patent leather Sherpa bag and most of his wardrobe. The red turtleneck sweater with the yellow, blue and green swirls was still his favorite piece of apparel, and fit him perfectly.

He really did not plan on looking at toys, but when he saw a latex squeak caterpillar named Daisy, he just could not resist. Daisy had six green legs, each with their own squeaker, a blue body, and a bulbous orange head with two yellow antennae and prominent white eyes. He thought Daisy would go well with Flutter, the latex squeak butterfly toy that Millie had given him, when he was a young puppy. After all, he reasoned, a caterpillar is merely the precursor of the butterfly, once removed by the process of metamorphosis.

Next he turned his attention to the accessories section. With the help of his human mommy and daddy, he tried on hats, kerchiefs, visors and sunglasses. It was a difficult choice, but he narrowed it down to a sun visor in an abstract black, yellow and white print. It fit him perfectly, had an adjustable chin strap, and from a practical standpoint, would shield the sun from his eyes.

The last purchases of the day were an insulated portable water canteen and a collapsible plastic food dish. Boomerang was ready to embark on the journey, and especially eager to find out more about the red rock country, which was still surrounded by an air of mystery.

That night, Boomerang visited with Grandpa Gem up in Heaven. He told his grandpa all about the upcoming journey, and asked him about the mysterious phrase.

Grandpa Gem nodded wisely and

said, "Before I begin, please promise me you will always remember: It's not the destination...it's the journey."

Boomerang's expression was solemn when he declared, "I promise you, grandpa, I'll always remember."

"Very well then, I will answer your question. Red rock country is a fantasy-land of wild beauty, spectacular vistas and majestic rock formations from thousands of years ago."

Boomerang listened intently as his grandpa continued the explanation.

"The red rocks are a mighty spectacle. They are exquisitely beautiful, a dramatic natural wonder. Nearby, you will also see incredible iridescent waterfalls, shimmering turquoise pools and flowering orchards. It's exceptionally breathtaking and very much like Heaven. There's even a lookout area up at the canyon called Bright Angel Point. Try to go there, if at all possible."

Boomerang was more than satisfied with the amount of information. Grandpa

Gem never ceased to amaze him with the extensive scope of his knowledge and the quickness of his recall. The red rock country sounded like a land of intense aesthetic pleasure -- breathtakingly beautiful, with magnificent red rock vistas and towering canyons. What a fantastic opportunity, thought Boomerang, to experience nature's spectacular artistry. This is going to be an unforgettable journey!

"Grandpa, thank you for all the helpful information. I love you so much."

Grandpa Gem beamed with pride. "Send my regards to Junior and the rest of the crows when you next see them. Tell them I said hello, and that I expect to rendezvous at their portal when the aspects are in harmonious alignment," he said with a twinkle in his eyes.

"I'll be sure to tell them, grandpa."

Grandpa Gem's aura expanded and merged with Boomerang's. They were both bathed in the ecstatic warmth of mutual and unconditional love. In that moment their hearts and minds blended into

Boomerang — A Miracle Trilogy

one entity. Boomerang was serene and content, knowing that their soul connection was forever, and could never be broken by space or time. He fondly remembered one of the first lessons Grandpa Gem had taught him back on Earth. Through love, all things are possible, even miracles!

Before departing, Boomerang told Grandpa Gem about his experiences on the bridge to the 21st century. Grandpa Gem promised to meet him at the bridge next time, so they could share the panoramic view together. Boomerang was overjoyed.

"Incidentally, there's an Angel in your future," Grandpa Gem said in a most nonchalant manner. Then he was gone, except for his halo.

What a cryptic message. Boomerang was intrigued by this latest revelation. He was filled with questions when he returned back to Earth.

Part 2

The Voyage

All is flux, nothing stands still.

-- Heraclitus (ca. 500 B.C.)

FOUR

Boomerang was packed and ready. He sat by the kitchen window, looking out for the limousine. The sky was cloudless, the sun was shining brightly, and there was a slight breeze in the air. It was the perfect day for a trip.

He kissed and hugged Mommy Crystal and Sister Penelope good-bye. They wished him a bon voyage. They would both miss him very much, but were glad to be staying home.

The doorbell rang. Boomerang's human daddy picked him up and carried him outside. Parked in their circular driveway was the most beautiful white limousine Boomerang had every seen. The bags were placed in the trunk, and they all piled into the spacious rear seat. His human mommy placed him in the Sherpa bag as a safety precaution, and she attached the seatbelt to the shoulder strap. They were finally enroute to the airport. Their vacation had officially begun!

Boomerang had met with Junior and the rest of the flock yesterday to say good-bye. He relayed Grandpa Gem's message about a "rendezvous at their portals," and he told Junior about the cryptic comment regarding his future.

"Another Angel ... Is that really what he said? Hmmm, let me see." Junior chuckled mischievously and scratched the glossy black feathers on top of his head. He stretched his wings fully and pretended to give it some thought. "Sounds to me like your grandpa might have some privileged information. He loves you very much, so you can be sure his intentions are purely innocent."

It was obvious that Junior was being intentionally evasive. Junior yawned casually and then, looking Boomerang straight in the eye, he continued speaking. "You know I love you like a brother, and I want whatever's best for your welfare. Can you try to be a little more patient, and wait for the future to unfold at its own pace? Remember, everything manifests at the appropriate moment. If we try to alter the natural succession of events, we also alter the course of destiny in an unnatural and artificial manner."

At least Junior is being honest with me. "Thank you. I understand your position and appreciate your honesty, but can you give me just a tiny little hint?" persisted Boomerang. He could be very determined at times , but Junior was not easily persuaded. He had learned to be very firm when necessary.

Corbie, who had been nodding his head in silent agreement as Junior talked, spoke up. "If we reveal what you want to know before the appropriate time, it could affect your future in a detrimental fashion. Not only will it interfere with your own destiny, but it can also change the entire outcome of your current mission on Earth and the success of the Kindness Network. Is that a risk you are willing to take?"

Boomerang shook his head emphatically. "Definitely not!" My mission on Earth has top priority. My first allegiance is to the Angel Connection, and my primary responsibility is to assure the success of the Kindness Network. I couldn't risk that for the sake of satisfying my own curiosity."

"Good," replied Corbie. "I'm so glad that's been settled. Now, what would you like to know about the red rock country?"

Boomerang was startled by Corbie's inquiry. Introspective by nature, Corbie only discussed matters that he considered to be of utmost importance. He rarely spoke, unless he had something pertinent to say. Otherwise, he merely listened and analyzed, as philosophers often do. Boomerang admired Corbie for his ability to remain calm and patient under all circumstances. It was a great comfort that he could always rely on Corbie to be rational and thoughtful.

He could also rely on all the crows for their uncanny ability to know everything about everything. Whether or not he told them, they always seemed to know.

Boomerang marveled at their all-knowing omniscient abilities, and he respected their vast knowledge. Most of all, he appreciated their loyal friendship. He always enjoyed their friendly banter, and he never minded their good-natured teasing.

They proceeded to fill him in about the sights he could expect to see while on vacation in the red rock country. Grandpa Gem had been quite thorough, but the crows elaborated even further. They described the medicine wheels, hot air balloon rides and jeep tours in great detail. Corbie suggested he visit some of the New Age bookshops, while Junior told him the vortex areas were not to missed.

"What's a vortex?" asked Boomerang.

"You'll see," said Junior with a mysterious wink, He wished Boomerang a bon voyage and flew off without another word. Corbie was nowhere to be seen. He had vanished into the trees.

Oh well, I guess I'll learn more about vortexes on my own, when the time

217

is right. Boomerang came out of his reverie just as the limousine arrived at the airport. They were well ahead of schedule. After checking the luggage at the ticket counter, there would be plenty of opportunity to explore the terminal prior to take-off.

When his flight's departure was announced, Boomerang and his human mommy and daddy were permitted to board the plane first. He was comfortably curled up in his Sherpa bag under the seat, before the other passengers began to embark.

The take-off was exhilarating, and the flight was smooth as silk. Midway through, the flight attendant approached Boomerang's human mommy and daddy, asking if they would like to take him out of the Sherpa bag for a while so he could stretch his legs and look out the window. Their answer, of course, was affirmative.

Boomerang admired the fluffy white cloud formations set against a bright blue sky. For a moment, his thoughts were

Boomerang — A Miracle Trilogy

transported back to Heaven. They were flying miles above the Earth, cushioned on a sea of air. It all seemed so effortless as the plane continued on its course to the final destination -- the red rock country. They were flying at a high velocity, as the forces of kinetic energy and inertia acted upon the plane and its many occupants. Boomerang could sense the wind rushing past the plane's sleek silver exterior, yet the only discernible sound was the soothing hum of the engines. Boomerang was lulled into a deep dreamless sleep.

The next thing he knew, there was a soft thud. Then a second thud. He awoke with a start. He realized it must be the landing gear. They were no longer flying high above the clouds. Boomerang peered out the window. He had a clear view of the town below. There were grids of streets, scattered houses separated by large patches of green grass, and a few moving vehicles.

His human mommy placed him back in the cozy Sherpa bag under the seat, in preparation for landing. Boomerang felt a wave of anticipation course through his entire body. The plane landed smoothly, as if gliding over glass, and the pilot taxied to the gate.

Boomerang, along with his human mommy and daddy, were the first passengers off the plane. He was filled with excitement, and eager for the future to unfold. They were about to embark on a journey filled with incredible beauty, unique mysticism and all the scenic wonders of nature -- a miracle odyssey into the red rock country. As they all headed for the baggage carousel, Boomerang clearly remembered Grandpa Gem's words of wisdom: "It's not the destination...it's the journey."

FIVE

The ride from the airport lasted over two hours, but the time passed quickly. Boomerang's human mommy and daddy listened to music on the car radio while he nestled in his fleece lined Sherpa bag. They watched the unspoiled desert terrain, and enjoyed the unusual scenery. The land was completely flat, and there were large open expanses of sandy soil and sagebrush.

The cactus growing along the highway came in all shapes and sizes, in various shades of green, from very dark to a pale chartreuse. Some of the cacti also produced bright blossoms, in shades of red, orange and yellow. The largest cactus, according to the guidebook, was of the saguaro variety. The giant saguaro was indigenous to the area and could grow up to a majestic sixty feet in height. After seventy-five years, the tall columnar trunk of the cactus would begin to form arms, finally maturing to its full size after one hundred and fifty years. From a distance, these cactus began to take on the form of a human figure, if one used a little imagination.

As the miles passed, the ground was gradually changing in appearance from taupe-colored desert to red-hued earth. Off in the distance could be seen mountains topped by snowy peaks. Outcroppings of red rocks were becoming visibly apparent against the backdrop of an azure blue desert sky. The contrast was strikingly beautiful. The topography had changed from flat desert to rolling grassland. As the elevation increased to over seven thousand feet above sea level, the temperature became noticeably cooler. The highway markers, posted at regular intervals, kept them informed of their increasing elevation, while the electronic overhead bulletin boards indicated the local time and the current outdoor temperature.

They continued driving toward the foothills of the mountains. Gradually, they began to see distant glimpses of deep gorges, embellished with enormous natural stone sculptures. Then, without warning, a broad canyon emerged, decoratively carved from colossal red sandstone walls. The canyon broadened, overshadowed by gigantic rock formations of red and orange that contrasted dramatically with the deep blue of the sky overhead. Fantastic shapes of spires and buttes brought sighs of amazement from Boomerang's human mommy and daddy.

They exited the highway and were approaching the hotel via a two lane roadway with no shoulder. The resort itself was just a short distance off the main highway, but only accessible by a long, narrow cobblestone driveway that twisted and turned through the rugged topography. The hotel was sequestered on over fifty acres, and consisted of two-story buildings clustered around a series of courtyards and walkways. The buildings were surrounded by landscaped gardens, and the atmosphere was serenely beautiful. The saguaro-studded landscape was dotted with natural outcroppings of massive red colored boulders.

A stately main building housed the reception area, lobby and several restaurants. Its coral stone facade was flanked by a pair of classic fluted fountains. The antique copper had aged to a fine patina, and reflected the setting sun with a soft glow. While Boomerang's human daddy checked in at the reception area, his human mommy gathered an additional supply of tour brochures at the concierge desk.

The hotel suite offered all the comforts of home. The accommodations were spacious and decorated with eclectic furnishings in neutral earth tones. The tall windows revealed awesome outdoor vistas. From the upstairs balcony, Boomerang could observe the fiery red cliffs of the rock formations, without any obstructions. The scene was spectacular. His gaze was riveted on the dramatic display before him. Boomerang was mesmerized. I'm officially immersed in the red rock country, he thought. The landscape is even more beautiful than I had imagined. I wish Grandpa Gem could be here to share the journey with me. Maybe someday. He was so engrossed in the scene, he was unaware that his human mommy had joined him on the balcony. She gave him a big hug and kisses. He reciprocated enthusiastically. They watched the sunset together.

Eventually, she helped him unpack

Boomerang — A Miracle Trilogy

and settle in. He had brought only his favorite toys along with him on vacation -- Daisy, the caterpillar; Flutter, the butterfly; and of course Big Kahuna, a gift which he had received on the first birthday of his prior lifetime. There was also his large imitation lambskin rug, which could double as a spare bed, his portable water canteen and collapsible food dish. The weather was expected to be seasonally warm and dry during the day, so the insulated canteen would come in handy. His human mommy had read it was so important to keep your body well-hydrated in dry climates, especially at high elevations. They had also packed his new visor hat, to shield his eyes from the bright glare of the sun and protect his head from the direct rays.

After everybody unpacked, Boomerang cuddled on the couch with his human mommy and daddy, while they perused the tour brochures obtained from the lobby. There were so many possibilities from which to choose. Among the choices were: hot-air balloon rides, white water rafting, helicopter tours into the canyon, and even skydiving! There were antique railroads, old castles, exquisite waterfalls, and cascading mountain streams. Nearly every form of recreation imaginable was available.

The brochures recommended exploring the red rock country by jeep, either independently or with a professional tour guide. A jeep, it seems, could navigate over the roughest terrain and access the most remote areas. In order to transverse the rugged topography and view the steep red cliffs up close, a four-wheel drive vehicle such as a jeep was the most practical mode of transportation.

After some discussion, they decided to take a leisurely approach and plan their sightseeing itinerary accordingly. There would be plenty of time before Millie arrived, and no need to rush. Boomerang's human mommy and daddy preferred to initially explore the red rock fantasyland on their own. Then, perhaps they could hire a guide later in the week.

Boomerang — A Miracle Trilogy

According to one of the brochures, there were many New Age bookstores in the area, since the red rock country attracted metaphysical students from all over the world. They were seeking spiritual growth and guidance. It seems the area was internationally famous for its dense concentrations of spiritual energy and highly charged electro-magnetic force fields.

These students attended lectures on spiritual development, meditation, healing circles, medicine wheels, crystal power, Kirlian photography, and other related subjects. Often the students become so involved with their metaphysical studies, they extended their visit much longer than originally intended. Some even stayed on permanently and eventually became teachers.

The red rock country was considered to be one of the foremost places in the world for those seeking a personal spiritual journey. Then it naturally follows, thought Boomerang, that as the new millenium approached and the expanded collective consciousness became more spiritually aligned in their awareness, the area would attract more and more visitors. Wow, what a perfect time to be experiencing a journey through the red rock country! This is all so amazing, and I am so very fortunate. Now, it's easy for me to understand Corbie's suggestion.

Boomerang's human mommy and daddy thought it might be worthwhile and interesting to visit at least one of the New Age bookshops, and obtain a schedule of classes. Boomerang agreed wholeheartedly. They all decided that would be their first excursion on the following day. Boomerang could hardly wait.

Boomerang — A Miracle Trilogy

Part 3

The Vortex

The most incomprehensible thing about the world, is that it is comprehensible.

-- Albert Einstein

SIX

The next morning Boomerang and his human mommy and daddy were all awake very early. It was partly due to jet lag -- they had flown three time zones to the west and their bodies were still adjusting. However, it was mostly because they were all so eager to begin their adventurous journey through the red rock country. Boomerang wished to explore and gather as much information as possible, especially anything pertaining to vortexes.

The first priority of the day was to visit a New Age bookstore. As it turned out, there was one located just past their hotel on the opposite side of the road. It was a small free-standing building, painted a pale shade of yellow. The window boxes were filled with assorted flowers, and the wind chimes hanging outside the front entrance were swaying in the gentle morning breeze. The initial impression was inviting and cheerful. They were the only customers in the shop, so the proprietor was able to devote her full attention to them. She greeted them warmly, and Boomerang responded with a big kiss hello. He appreciated the pleasant atmosphere, and he liked her immediately. Instinctively, he knew she was a sincere and kind person. Her eyes emanated genuine concern and her smile was captivating. Boomerang felt instantly connected to her.

"My you're a handsome fellow," she said to Boomerang and gave him a wink. Then she turned her attention to his human mommy and daddy. "My name is Ariel, and I'm the owner and manager of this establishment. Please tell me how I can be of service to you." She handed them her business card. The card was the same pale yellow color as the exterior of the building. They scanned the raised gold letters on the front of the card, which read: The New Age Center for Cosmic Enhancement.

Ariel had been standing beside a glass showcase filled with quartz crystals, both large and small, and an assortment of other talismans. She proceeded to give them a brief tour of the charming shop. The front room was lined with book shelves, from floor to ceiling. Ariel pointed out and explained the arrangement of the books by subject matter. Then she led them down a short hallway to the back of the store.

"We offer classes and workshops dealing with all aspects of spiritual development. The rear portion of the building is devoted exclusively to our seminars. Our instructors are experts in their chosen fields," she said with pride. "We've all worked very hard to maintain a sterling reputation."

They returned to the front room, and she handed them a schedule of classes for the week. The schedule listed the time of each class, a brief synopsis of the lecture topic, and the instructor's name and credentials. Boomerang's human mommy and daddy looked over the list. There were metaphysical classes offered in so many sub-specialties. The most interesting were:

meditation and past life regression, crystal healing, angelic healing, electro-magnetic field balancing, aura photos (Kirlian photography), and power vortexes.

"The majority of our students register well ahead of time. As a result, some of our classes this week are already full," Ariel apologized. "However, there are still some openings in Kirlian photography and meditation. Would either of those interest you?"

"What is Kirlian photography?" asked Boomerang's human mommy, uncertain if her pronunciation was correct.

"It is a method of photographing auras, using special infra-red equipment. An aura is a subtle emanation, visible as an elliptical sphere of white or colored light surrounding the physical body. We are actually able to photograph your aura, or electro-magnetic field, using specially designed two-layer metallic and glass photographic plates. The aura from living creatures appears to be related to the mental, emotional and physical health of the subject being photographed. Therefore the aura can be used to detect illness well before other symptoms appear. That's why Kirlian photography is sometimes referred to as plasma photography". Ariel paused for a moment and then she added, "The same technology can be used to photograph the etheric body of an angel. The visible results are what we refer to as a halo, which is actually the uppermost expanded part of the aura above the head and shoulders."

Boomerang had been listening to Ariel closely, and he knew what she said was absolutely true. Meanwhile, his human mommy and daddy asked Ariel to please tell them a little more about the meditation class.

"Our meditation class is really a workshop, and it is the first step in preparing for a past-life regression. We help you practice proper breathing and relaxation techniques. Most important, we teach you how to seal off your aura for maximum protection, before starting a meditation."

"Is the class suitable for beginners, or is it geared toward more advanced students?" asked Boomerang's human daddy.

"It's a very basic introductory class. However, you will learn a great deal. I highly recommend it, especially if you plan on continuing your metaphysical studies."

"We prefer not to leave Boomerang alone at the hotel. Will we be permitted to bring him with us?" they asked Ariel in unison.

"Of course, he's more than welcome in any of our lectures. In fact, if you like you can have his aura photographed during the Kirlian class, so you can visually see the current state of his health."

"That would be fantastic! It would certainly help my peace of mind, and it would be a great keepsake from our journey together." Boomerang's human mommy was so overcome with emotion, tears of happiness filled her eyes and flowed down her cheeks. Ariel reached under the counter and brought out a box of tissues. Boomerang was so touched, he began to cry also. Before long, there was not a dry eye in the shop.

Ariel understood completely. It was apparent how important Boomerang's well-being was to his human mommy and daddy, and how very much they loved him. The feeling was obviously mutual on Boomerang's part.

They registered for both classes. The meditation workshop was the following day, and the aura photography class was to be held later in the week. They thanked her profusely for being so helpful and patient. The store was beginning to fill up with other customers, and they certainly did not wish to monopolize her time.

However, as Boomerang and his human mommy and daddy were preparing to depart, one of the newcomers approached Ariel and asked her about the background of the red rock country.

"Where did all these red rocks come from?" he inquired. "Never seen anything quite like it," he admitted, "and I've traveled extensively."

237

"Having resided in this area my entire life, I would be happy to share what I know with you," she responded with unbridled enthusiasm.

People who had been scattered throughout the store, browsing the bookshelves, overheard the conversation and gradually gathered around Ariel as she began to explain the origins of the red rock country. Nearby, Boomerang was listening with rapt attention. He was totally engrossed and fascinated by the red rocks, and he wanted to know more.

Ariel, encouraged by all the sudden interest and attention, began an informal extemporaneous lecture concerning the history of the red rocks. As she surveyed the room, everybody was watching her expectantly and listening intently. When her gaze fell upon Boomerang, he was looking directly at her, his big brown eyes open wide, head cocked to one side, ears at full attention, as if to say, "Please tell me more, I'm listening attentively."

"The landscape in this area consists

primarily of rugged cliffs, needle like pinnacles and isolated buttes, which are hills with steep sides and flat tops. This ragged topography rises up from the green forest floor below, at the mouth of the canyon." She sipped from a bottle of mineral water before continuing. "The red rocks date back to prehistoric times. Layers of different-colored stone were deposited during the various prehistoric ages, forming bands through the cliffs above. The most prominent of these bands is the layer of red sandstone. Because this rosy sandstone predominates in this area, the entire region has come to be known as the red rock country. Each evening at sunset, the famous red rocks put on a light show all their own. Are there any questions...or shall I continue?"

Boomerang's human mommy raised her hand before speaking. "Yes, I have a question," she said. "Since there are so many red rocks in the area, and time really does not permit seeing all of them, are there any particular red rock formations you would recommend to a first-time visitor?"

"Yes, interestingly, some of the more popular red rock formations have even been given names, based upon their shape and size. There's Submarine Rock, Balancing Rock, Bell Rock, Eagle Head Rock, Mother and Child Rock, Snoopy Rock, and Cathedral Rock. Cathedral Rock happens to be the most photographed."

Ariel answered a few other questions, and she suggested some books for further reading on the subject.

"Whoever is interested in exploring the red rock country on their own, may obtain a complimentary detailed map at the local Chamber of Commerce down the road. The map will indicate the locations of the most popular rock formations, along with the four main power vortexes."

Boomerang's head shot up. Vortex -- there was that word again! That was the same term Junior had mentioned. He had told Boomerang the vortexes were not to be missed. But what are they? Boomerang hoped Ariel would explain, and he sent her a telepathic message, while he concentrated intensely. It worked like a charm!

"According to experts on the subject, a vortex is a site where the Earth's unseen lines of power converge. This intersection forms a particularly powerful energy field, technically called a high-energy electromagnetic force field. It has been determined there are four main vortex areas located in red rock country, and numerous smaller vortexes. In fact, many of the most spectacular rock formations also happen to be power vortexes."

Ariel paused a moment, and she looked at the clock over the door. Boomerang had been listening so intently, he had lost all track of time. She had been very patient with all the questions and interruptions. However, now she began to speak more rapidly, and Boomerang knew the impromptu lecture was coming to a close.

"Despite the physical beauty of the red rocks, this area is most famous for its vortex areas, where the Earth's cosmic energy fields converge. All vortexes are said to contain electromagnetic energy, which facilitates relaxation as well as healing, and balances emotional, spiritual and physical energy. This is why visitors from around the world are attracted to the area, seeking spiritual development and healing." As Ariel continued to speak, Boomerang could hear the sense of pride in her voice. "As word spread, large numbers of people came here to experience the power vortexes of the red rock country. We became popular as a sacred site for the New Age. Ultimately, we have evolved into one of the world's centers for the New Age movement, and we hope it continues well into the new millenium. Now, that concludes the mini-series for today," she said with a laugh. "I do hope you are all feeling cosmically enhanced."

Everybody applauded enthusiastically. Then the group dispersed in various directions. Boomerang's human mommy and daddy purchased a large volume on meditation in preparation of their class the following day, and a smaller book about vortexes and energy fields. They thanked Ariel once again, and they expressed admiration for the depth of her knowledge. Boomerang gave her a big kiss good-bye. In response, she chucked him under the chin, patted his head and said, "Bye-bye handsome. I certainly look forward to seeing you back here tomorrow."

Ah, that sounds great, he thought with satisfaction. He bestowed a series of kisses upon her, to express his appreciation of the kindness in her soul.

SEVEN

The remainder of the week passed very quickly for Boomerang and his human mommy and daddy. They attended the New Age lectures as planned; shopped for local souvenirs and trinkets; and toured an outdoor desert botanical garden, covering more than one hundred and fifty acres. They drove to a petrified forest, where the ancient wood had actually turned into colorful stone, and they enjoyed watching the nightly sunsets of deep orange. Boomerang was having the best vacation he could have ever imagined.

They visited a dormant volcanic crater that was approximately nine hundred years old. It rose one thousand feet in height with shades of red, orange and yellow cinders -- resembling a sunset -- leading to the summit. Boomerang admired the sweeping beauty and felt its mystical history. He also had the good fortune of accompanying his human mommy and daddy on a vintage steam-powered railway. Together, they rode all the way up to the canyon, where the views were absolutely spectacular! Just as Grandpa Gem had suggested, they stopped at a fantastic scenic overlook called Bright Angel Point where Boomerang posed for pictures. His eyes sparkled with pleasure, while his human mommy and daddy took numerous photos of him against the panoramic background of the mountains in the distance.

Boomerang — A Miracle Trilogy

One of the most amazing experiences of the week was the balloon adventure. Early one morning they ascended in a hot air balloon and leisurely drifted over the red rock country. The winds were calm and the temperature was cool. They were high above the ground, allowing for a spectacular view of the rock formations below. At first Boomerang thought he was dreaming. I am soaring through the air like a bird, he reflected, just like when the crows fly effortlessly over the treetops. It was even more exhilarating than flying above the clouds in an airplane. Here he was, enjoying the delightful scenery in a brightly colored hot air balloon at sunrise. After the awesome flight of about one hour, they enjoyed a traditional balloonist's champagne ceremony. Boomerang's human mommy and daddy sipped the champagne while he drank spring water from his travel canteen. They each received a personal first flight certificate, embossed with their names and the following sentiment: "There are few pleasures as grand as drifting slowly over the earth in an open basket. It's breathtaking. It's a journey you'll never forget..."

What a fantastic way to start the day, thought Boomerang. I cannot possibly imagine a more exciting excursion! Observing the red rocks from a height of three thousand feet had conveyed a whole new perspective to Boomerang. It was an important opportunity to see the effect of distance upon the appearance of objects; how the judgment of circumstances was determined by one's particular location and special point-of-view. Boomerang was deeply impressed. He remembered the solemn promise recently made to Grandpa Gem, and he thought about the words that were forever etched into his memory. "It's not the destination...it's the journey!"

Up to this point they had been exploring the red rock country on their own. Now, they were finally ready for a guided tour of the power vortexes. Boomerang was thrilled to join his human mommy and daddy on their first tour of the sacred sights. The guide drove the jeep over the